DEAR DONALD

To my dear friend
Gayle &
God Bless America

Love,
Sandra x

DEAR DONALD

LETTERS FROM A LOVING DEPLORABLE

SANDRA LEE

Dear Donald: Letters From A Loving Deplorable

Cover photo and design by Marc Anthony, www.marcandtony.com

Library of Congress Control Number available upon request

Print ISBN 978-0-9966208-3-3

eBook ISBN 978-0-9966208-4-0

Dedication

This book is dedicated to my wonderful friends and family, especially Laurie, Diane and Stuart who read and reacted to every page along the way. Their encouragement was awesome. Thank you to Alex for her insistence that writing is in the stars for me. Thank you to Dale, who cheers me on in sickness and in health, and to my precious children, my son, Dennis; daughter-in-law, Stacey; and grandchildren, Lucas and Trey, who are my inspiration. I hope I am honoring my parents who bravely educated their daughter in a time when educating daughters was a bold leap into the unknown.

Notes From the Author

Donald Trump has changed my life. I love writing. I have always written songs, poems, stories, articles, and plays. "The Donald" inspired me to write my first book. This man has held my attention captive for the last several years. I am not just listening, I am driven to listen, watch and observe every political and personal move. Why? Do I care more about my country than I ever have? I do.

I reminisce about politicians who would urge their voters to do the right thing for the sake of their children and grandchildren. I listened to those pleas and could not relate to them before I had children of my own. I am deeply concerned about the world that they are inheriting. I support Donald Trump's vision for our country, but there is more. He has inspired something remarkable in me. He seems ageless and tireless as he moves forward. When I feel old and tired, I watch him and shake off those negative feelings and embrace what is young and strong in me.

I juxtapose my life experience to his and find treasures of awareness. He has a past that is imperfect. There are mistakes...big ones. There are failures and disappointments. He lets them go. He sheds them like old skins. He is holy in ways that I am not sure many can articulate. It is easy to magnify his sins, but he is quick to point out his many successes. I watch him forgive himself for his sins and move on embracing that forgiveness. His energy and light are not dimmed by regret or remorse. He is born again moment by moment and so he receives a blessing of renewal. I watch in wonder and I learn.

HOME SWEET HOME

———————

January 1, 2017

Dear Donald,

From the porch of my little house on a hill in Port Washington, on Long Island, I had a clear view of the Manhattan skyline. I remember admiring the twin towers from that porch the morning of 9/11 and noting how blue and beautiful the sky was. I took in a deep breath and happily drove off to teach my seventh graders who were scheduled that day for a lesson in the school library. The kids and I scurried around the library piling up books on study tables. They enjoyed hunting for their favorites and needed to sign them out before the bell rang. The televisions were on in the library that morning and the children were gathering and then flocking around them in awe. What was going on? I couldn't get them to settle down. We huddled and stared in shock for more time than I remember, at airplanes flying into towers and towers crumbling to the ground.

I spent the day trying to keep the children from panic. Televisions were on throughout the school. Parents were streaming in all day to take their children home. At last, I was able to locate my son and head back to the house. We stood on the front porch and gazed at the skyline which had completely changed. New York City, I feared, would never recover from this blow. For many years after 9/11, it was not a city of bright lights and glamour to me, until the year that you and Melania glided down the iconic escalator at Trump Towers and you announced that you were running for President. "All the kings horses and all the king's men" couldn't put New York back together again in my broken heart. But, something about that smooth and confident decent from your Tower of unending strength renewed my hope for the country that I loved and the city that was its crowning jewel.

You never gave up on New York City. You had given so much of your life to it. New Yorkers never forgot how you refurbished the Wollman Skating Rink in Central Park. The city had spent twelve million dollars and years trying to get that job done and they failed. You took it on and got it done in six months, two and a half months ahead of your schedule and seven hundred fifty thousand dollars below your three million dollar budget.

The Trump Towers in cities around the world have made you famous. I left New York and came back to Ohio after 9/11. You stayed, continuing glamorous reconstruction, like the restoration of the stately Commodore Hotel. That project was instrumental in cleaning up the street prostitution that had become common on Park Avenue. Many of us were giving up on New York. We were walking out. You were walking in. You were determined to make it and America great again.

ELLIS ISLAND

January 2, 2017

Dear Donald,

I spoke to my cousin Robbie Today. Her name is Rabiah in Arabic. She speaks more French than Arabic. My father was born near Beirut, Lebanon in Zahale and he also spoke French. Robbie tells me that all of her family in Lebanon urged her to vote for you. The Christians in the Middle East are worried about their future. Many were extremely unhappy about the last eight years of Barack Obama's leadership in the United States. Her family would call from overseas and urge her to vote for that man who came down the escalator. That iconic escalator! I knew the minute I saw that image with you and Melania that the future was certain. Yes, you were going to change the world and that America would be great again!

I did what I could for you where I live in Ohio. I went to the family car dealership to lease a new Lincoln as my Jaguar was ten years old. It was time to make a change. Really. Matthew McConaughey had been doing Lincoln commercials. They were so glamorous that I was willing to part from my "Jag" to, at last, drive my family signature car since my return to Cleveland over fifteen years ago.

Driving from the dealer parking lot in my new Lincoln MKC, I noticed a Trump campaign office down the street. It was a small storefront and not very impressive. I drove into the lot, went in and signed up to volunteer for you! I had never done that before for any other candidate. However, I always voted. I was not very politically involved or active. But, I, like many other Americans, felt called to this in spite of the negative news media.

People seem to resent you because of your wealth. "Rich" is not a dirty word to me. When money comes from hard work and capitalizing on opportunities of the American dream, I am OK with it. I would like to be a billionaire.

My dad came from Lebanon when he was eighteen. He married my mother who was his first cousin. They stayed married for a lifetime. My mom was born here. Some of his family could not get into the country. He worshiped America. So often I would hear him say, "What a country!" He saw opportunity and worked eighteen hours a day. First, as a cab driver, then in an auto body repair shop. He ended up buying the body shop and sold some used cars that he restored. Later, he secured a Lincoln Mercury franchise, built a dealership, built a bigger one and there you have it. The American dream. Growing up, I wore a lot of red, white and blue.

Ellis Island was the dream of many people. They made the long journey to the land of milk and honey and hard work in search of more for themselves and their families. My dad was one of those. To commemorate his journey to citizenship and hard work, I bought him a stone to add to the wall at Ellis Island. When

I visited, I couldn't find it on the computer location service. I roamed around outside and looked at all of the other names. I stopped to gaze at Lady Liberty, that beautiful statue, on that warm summer day. When I turned my head, there was his stone. I cried. God led me right to it. Perhaps it was my dad in heaven that identified it for me! This effort to place his stone at Ellis Island was one of the most patriotic things I have ever done. That, and walking into the Trump campaign office down the road from my dad's dealership.

BIRTHDAY

January 5, 2017

Dear Donald,

You honor your children from three marriages. For those of us who have been married and divorced, your past is not so shocking. I am sad to see how divorce has disrupted the family structure in our country. I long for "the good old days" when Sunday dinners with grandparents, aunts and uncles, cousins and kids were the norm.

After I was divorced, my son's father met a young woman, and she became pregnant with their child. She did not want to continue the relationship, but she did want the child. She requested that he have no contact with this child and he honored that request. I knew nothing about this relationship until that child, whose name is Brooke, was an adult. Her mother married when Brooke was very young and never told Brooke about her real father. When Brooke's step father revealed to her the he was not her real father, but that her real father was alive, Brooke was, of course shocked and curious. She bravely sought to connect with her real father.

When my adult son shared all of this with me, my first concern was to handle the news and the situation in a way that would be most supportive of him. I was pleased to see that my son was open, accepting, and excited to welcome his half sister into his life. We lived in New York at the time and Brooke lived in Florida. A meeting was planned and I made a firm decision to embrace this young woman with love. It was easy. She was sweet, brilliant, beautiful and talented. She was fun. She and my son bonded immediately and have remained close for years.

Donald, I think that your imperfect past, which was endlessly thrown in your face during the election, is part of why I like you so much. Most of us have done plenty that we are not proud of, or our immediate family has, and we hold ourselves back because we don't feel worthy of success or love or whatever. We are brave and forge ahead climbing the ladders in spite of it all, but there is something holding us back. Our past haunts us deep down in our subconscious and we can't let ourselves reach our potential.

You give me hope. It seems that you are able to accept yourself and love yourself unconditionally. You don't make a big deal of your mistakes and you don't let the criticisms of others get to you. You focus on what is working and you think you are just great and so you are. You believe America can be greater than ever! So you have Americans believing that no matter what mess we are in, it's no big deal. You teach us to tear it down, dig it up, reinvent, dress it up in gold, make it shine and claim the day!

Brooke is a bright spot in my life. You might say that I "Donaldized" her. She is great. Everything is just great if I say so, and I do. I choose to love her in this complicated situation because she is really lovable. She gets me. Even though she is not my daughter and I have to share my son with her, I benefit. She is another way to connect with my son, her half brother. She is a part of his father, who, no matter what our differences were, is a man I will always love.

A WAKE AND AWAKE

January 8, 2017

Dear Donald,

My companion, Dale, and I just got back from a wake. The place was packed and the lines were very long to pay respects to the family. Had we stayed, we would have waited in line for over an hour. No way. We barely knew the deceased, but I am a good friend of his sister so we wanted to make an appearance. I felt frustrated, angry and upset with myself for having negative feelings about this crowded event. I started to wonder if anyone would care if I died. I couldn't imagine a mob scene to honor me. I wondered just exactly how many lives I had impacted and who would even miss me if I were gone. To think about this was my personal "great awakening.

Donald, you might be a very controversial figure, but trust me, your wake will be packed. I know you are having a rough time with Hollywood regarding the Inaugural Ball. That has to hurt just a little. Don't forget the ten, fifteen, twenty plus thousand people who showed up to support you state after state. Hollywood might show up to bid you farewell, as well as your many friends, colleagues and fans. Not to mention all of us grieving at home remembering all you did for our country. You are all set.

I have friends, relatives, former students, readers and viewers of my former TV show as well as four major relationships in the last many years. Surely, there are neighbors, people from church, community meetings, friends at my condo in Florida, my Ohio family, my son and grandsons who might attend my funeral. Would any of them show up for me? I guess some would.

Dale couldn't relate to my upset. He said, "Who cares? You will be dead." Oh, to be like Dale, with a "what difference does it make" attitude. No muss, no fuss, no bother.

I have done a million meaningful things and somehow, I don't believe they've amounted to much. Either my thinking is distorted or I had better get moving. Debbie Reynolds and her daughter left so many concrete memories. Those two left movies, books, songs, plays and pictures. Their memories will linger.

Obama is going nuts trying to preserve his legacy. I get it. He did his best. And whether I like it or not is beside the point. He wants to be remembered, appreciated and honored.

I want to be free of this endless wanting. I want, I want, I want. I want to want nothing. It's exhausting to want so much. Maybe I just want to be sitting on the beach wearing nothing but a smile. Even wanting to not want is still wanting.

Can you find a member of your cabinet to solve this circuitous problem? I am busy getting dizzy.

SYLVIA

————

January 9, 2017

Dear Donald,

My cleaning lady, Sylvia, understands you. We both watched the Golden Globe Awards last night. I didn't catch what Meryl Streep had to say about you until this morning when Sylvia told me. I learned that you said Meryl was "highly overrated as an actress." Donald, how do you get away with this stuff? I actually laughed even though I don't agree with you. I can't stand her politics but I have been impressed with her career and the roles she has played. She is so versatile and inventive. You are not diplomatic Donald. I can't believe you really think that about her. Your "no diplomacy" attitude is refreshing. I have mastered the art of diplomacy and it was hard work. You just spit out whatever is on your mind, no filters. Your way is deliciously dangerous.

Sylvia comes to the house every other week for four hours. I have a very large home and I can't keep up with the housework. It is so wonderful to have the extra help. Luckily, my guy Dale, is a big help. Between the three of us, the house is always in order.

————

Maybe not the kind of order your house is in, but in enough order for me.

My mom had help with cleaning when I was growing up. That was quite a luxury. Our cleaning lady was black and worked for us for over ten years. We loved Annie. She took the bus and got off at the stop across from our Tudor style home in Lakewood, Ohio. It looks a little like the town you grew up in on Long Island. I've driven in your old neighborhood and it reminded me of home.

Annie would arrive all dressed up and descend to the basement to change into her house dress in the bathroom. It was an unfinished bathroom with a cracked concrete wall and floor. It was chilly in the basement in the winter. I asked my mother to let her change in the lavatory on the first floor in the back hallway. Prejudice is unnatural to young children. Sometimes they just say what they think. If you had this loving time with a kind woman for years and years, you sure don't want her changing in a dingy cold room.

Donald, sometimes I think you are crazy. Other times I am so relieved that you are in charge. It is irrational, but sometimes your "get it done" attitude makes me feel unsafe. And then, strangely, I change to the "burn the house down if you have to but save the baby" state of mind.

Sylvia and I are both hard working people who have spent a lot of our years as single mothers. We are counting on you. We believe in you. I guess we are all ready to roll up our sleeves and clean house. Together, with God's help, we will "drain the swamp."

Sylvia just said, "Move over Meryl, Donald is about to play his biggest role."

LATE NIGHTS

———

January 12, 2017

Dear Donald,

There is no doubt that you are an inspiration. It is well after five and I am still working as hard and as fast as I can. I have this relentless spirit to push harder than usual and to expect more of myself. You are so energized and I loved watching as you went from city to city, from one huge event to another during the campaign. You are not afraid of work, and yet, I do not see you as a workaholic. You couldn't have the amazing relationships with your children if you didn't make time to engage them and be their dad.

I think work is your music, building is your poetry and solving challenging problems is your inspiration. I am writing five books at a time and my son is losing patience with me. He said to me today, "Mom, just write one and finish one." But then I learned that Danielle Steele wrote five books at a time. Perhaps I am the next Danielle Steele!

Last night, I spent about forty-five minutes on FaceTime with my son and grandsons. Lucas, who is eleven, asked me to study with him for his history test. Trey, my seven-year-old grandson, demonstrated the features of the bunk beds that I bought for the boys. I have seen this demonstration many times. He wants to be sure that I understand the exceptional features of his monster hero ZippySac. He even stages commercials for it. One time, he was in the grocery store with his mom and he burst into a commercial for turkeys. He held one up and exclaimed how incredible it was.

I am telling you all of this because I am obsessed with my children. My son and my grandchildren are most important to me. I also love my work and I am consumed with it. Maybe it is passion. I prefer that. You seem so passionate about your work, your family, beautiful women and making America great again.

I loved that Obama gave Joe Biden that medal today. I loved that Joe cried tears of joy when he received it. They surely had an adventure together. I didn't care what history finally says, I voted for you Donald. I also believe that Obama and Biden did their best promoting their political ideology.

It is such an amazing accomplishment to become President or Vice President of the United States. Obama and Biden inspire me and so do you. I am working as hard as I can to do all the things that are in my heart to do. I am pushing harder than ever even at my age. I should be slowing down, but I am speeding up because I have to accomplish what is on my very long list.

There are a lot of songs in my heart. For a while, I would open my mouth but the energy and passion to sing a note was not there. You have me singing again. Thank you.

SEVENS

Dear Donald,

My pastor has been presenting a series of sermons based on the number seven. It is significant in the structure of the Bible and the universe. Today is the seventeenth day of the year 2017. My birthday is on the 17th day of the seventh month of the year. I feel like something very significant or intensely lucky should happen today. I bought a lottery ticket. If I win, the jackpot is over one hundred fifty million and of course, there are the taxes. I try to imagine multiplying that amount by the huge number it would take to get to your net worth. It is astounding, yet, I try.

I am working on expanding my prosperity consciousness. I cannot pull out the rocking chair like my peers, because I am still working on building a fortune. The wealth building you have done is staggering! You are going to be President of the United States in the year of my lucky number, seventeen! This gives me the most delightful feeling of good fortune.

At the same time, the world seems to be falling apart. Forty

---

members of Congress are refusing to go the Inauguration this week. I am sorry. Your rough style got you elected. Fairness is not always gentle. You can be so brash. I think about Zen masters who shout at their devotees. Even Jesus expressed temper at the Temple. There is a lot of temper going around right now and only time will hopefully end it.

In a few minutes, my friend Denise, is picking me up to go to a benefit lunch at a club for educators. This minuscule act of charity is dwarfed by the enormous gestures you make at improving the lives of millions of Americans. I am pushing myself to give more time, money and thoughtfulness. I sense the generous hearts of you and your family, and I am stirred.

Thanks to television, I know what you are doing every single day. I remember one of my first exposures to television was when I sadly watched American soldiers returning from Korea. They looked sad, disheveled, thin and distant. There are too many problems across the globe. Thank you for being willing to take them on.

I offer my respectful farewell to the Obamas and my sincere congratulations and best wishes to you and your family. May the year 2017 mark the beginning of a blessed time for us all.

BROCCOLI CHEDDAR

January 18, 2017

Dear Donald,

Today, I feel more frustrated than inspired by you. I think it is because you are so rich and your life seemingly so perfect. I can't attain what you have. The women in your life are so beautiful and so fit. I am sure they are consistent in their work schedules and self-care. I find myself reaching for the stars and pushing to get things done. Then I am exhausted. I don't think about exercising or what I eat, although it is always on my mind. I find myself eating broccoli cheddar cheese soup, corn bread and a Ruben sandwich with chips. I will also share with you that my day began with a trip to Dunkin' Donuts for a large coffee with cream and of course, a donut. One minute I am on track and looking and feeling really good. The next, I am refusing to count calories, get on the scale or try on clothes.

Unknowingly, you have set the bar too high for me. Everyone in the cabinet is filthy rich, excessively accomplished and overly brilliant. I am energized to reach towards my goals and dwarfed

----

at the same time. I did all of my homework in school. I was class valedictorian and gave the commencement speech which was entitled "Climb Every Mountain." The message was inspired by the song from *The Sound of Music.*I was young, motivated and ready to climb. I was off to college to pave the way for climbing mountains.

Today, there are still mountains to climb and streams to ford. But at my age, things are different. I want to do it all. I sometimes feel scattered. One minute I am selling and building and creating. The next, I am wondering if I have lost my mind. Maybe I should just go to the condo and retire like women my age are supposed to do.

My father was ambitious and successful. I didn't have what you had. In years gone by, fathers pushed their sons to achieve. You encouraged and supported you sons and your daughters to achieve. My mother pushed a little but was not convinced that a girl should get carried away with ambitions. My father didn't have sons and it never occurred to him to groom his daughter to take over his business. I want to leap to your level. Sadly, time is not on my side for the necessary small steps that must be taken. This will take longer than the years I have left.

The country has a love/hate relationship with you. Should we worship you? Tear you down? Get behind you and support your efforts? Protest your strength? Be good soldiers? Celebrate your candor? Criticize you lack of tact? Be liberated by your lack of political correctness? Should we get on the "Trump train" or park a truck on the tracks? I'll bet that questions like these cross your mind every day. I think I know how you answered them.

We are both strong. Like Popeye, strong to the finish. You are giving your all and I will do the same. Where I end up is not the point, it is how I got there.

PROUD TO BE AN AMERICAN

January 19, 2017

Dear Donald,

I am happy for you today, the first day of the Inaugural celebrations. I am watching you at the Lincoln Memorial as we both listen to Lee Greenwood sing, "God Bless the USA." Bless him. It has been really difficult for entertainers to take on all of the post-election dissent. Lee is brave and talented and so moving when he sings his iconic song with such heart and pride. You jumped up to rush to the stage, hug the performers and to thank them. I know how grateful you were for their enthusiastic tribute to this historic event.

Washington has never looked so beautiful to me. I am enjoying the bright blue sky and the stunning array of your family members, one more beautiful and handsome than the next. The masses before you are jubilant and thrilled. The setting is historic and majestic. The country music is so American.

My modest participation in the election process has made a difference in my sense of investment in my country. I am proud to be an American and grateful that my son and his family will enjoy the protection here. Tomorrow, you will be sworn in. God is good. I am praying for you today, for all of those loyal Americans who are there with you and for those who are watching on television. I even pray for the people who, for whatever reasons, felt the need to stay away. This is a free country and no one is forced to bow down to any leader. I feel confident that you will win them over in time. You are brilliant at winning.

Yesterday, I felt exhausted, defeated and jealous of your stamina and enthusiasm. Today, I worked so hard at creating and producing. In spite of it all, I continue to push forward. Whatever is in me will be played out. That is my pledge to you today. I will write until my computer burns out. I will act and produce and create as long as there is an idea in my head or a desire in my heart. I will be confident and follow my gut feelings and not doubt them. You are relentless and following your lead, I refuse to buckle. If you can keep going, so can I. Today, working on my magazine was fun and working with my staff was a delight. The day was full with friends, activity, affection and optimism.

There is a little secret in my heart that I must keep private when out and about. I do not want to offend those who are not happy today. I want to shout, but I am only brave enough to whisper, HOORAY! Maybe someday, the ones who felt they lost the election will calm down, grow up and enjoy the benefits of your leadership.

CONFIDENCE

———

January 23, 2017

Dear Donald,

You look happy! As usual, the TV is on and it will be all day. It's Monday, your first real work day and you are meeting with union people. The press secretary held the first press conference, all the marches have stopped and the work of our President has begun.

I am happy too, but not nearly as confident as you. It has been a difficult economy for small businesses for a very long time. The change that I am experiencing in the market is either a mirage or a blessing. I have to say that my clients are optimistic and confident about their future. They are investing in themselves with an attitude of certainty, which is refreshing.

The profits seem real and my spirit of giving is expanding. Today, on television, you ordered your people to write a ten thousand dollar check to a loyal young supporter. This young man had never owned a suit and friends helped him to buy one to travel to Washington. The young man had a sick father who had cancer.

———

I am writing more and more checks to charities. I made a pledge to my church to tithe ten percent of my income before taxes. I have been doing that for fifteen months. This is a spiritual experiment. As I give, I look for blessings. Recently, I have noticed an increase in confidence. This makes me a more effective business woman. I am more focused on my career and singing.

There is so much criticism about you. It has been said that you are not qualified for the office you hold and you should be removed. Your sordid past comes to haunt you and the media goes wild. You don't seem to wince. I guess you know better of your qualifications and plans. I have moved from relentless defense of you to occasional concern. How much of you is real and how much is smoke? I wonder about myself, how much of this new lease on life is reasonable and how much is pure folly?

Here I am with a real magazine, real life savings, a real home, a real vacation home, a real car, real health, zeal, enthusiasm and hundreds of real written pages for my several books in process. Some smoke and some mirrors, indeed! But as I believe my exaggerated hype, I produce results. I am selling myself to myself all of the time. We are alike in that way. Sell it. Going once, going twice...sold.

DREAMING

January 25, 2017

Dear Donald,

Are you dreaming? You're going to build a wall on the border, straighten out the crime in Chicago, investigate illegal voting, fill the Cabinet, bring jobs back to America and get China, Russia, Syria, North Korea, Iran and Israel figured out. You are ambitious.

Mary Tyler Moore died today. She was 80. You and I are not so far away from that number! Yet, we stubbornly refuse to act our ages. There are times when I want to say to you, "Grow up!" The truth is, I don't want you to change a hair for me, not if you care for me.

I am running two homes, keeping up with my son and grandchildren who are five hundred miles away, writing five books and publishing a magazine. I haunt the choir director at church to help me learn a few songs to sing a solo. I also run back and forth to the recreation center to use the hot water pool for therapy to rehabilitate after my second hip replacement. I am also trying to forget last year's brain aneurism surgery and the

----

procedure for the spot on my heart. I think it was called an ablation. I should be looking at assisted living right now. I refuse to give in to that scene!

You do not act your age. You work eighteen hours a day and stay fresh and energetic. You keep telling yourself, and America, how great you are and we are beginning to believe it. I've known you were rich for a long time. Now, every day and night I see on television another mansion, hotel, penthouse or building. I even noted a ten thousand or one million dollar act of kindness! Is the money keeping you young, or, is it the climbing the mountains of challenges? Maybe it is the money you pay your staff to keep you in shape.

You haven't had any face lifts or cosmetic surgeries, have you? You are too busy conquering the world and are excited about your dreams. I am like that too, but I have some slumps. There are times when I think I should get a face lift. If my book takes off and I have to do television interviews, I had better be in good shape, primped and crimped, lifted and filled. I will simply refuse to accept the reality that is and invent a new one. I will be strong, invincible, healthy and look and act less than half my age. I will! I will! I will! I will make Sandra great again, greater than ever before.

ADDICTION

Dear Donald,

I really like Marie Osmond. But, I have to say that I am really tired of her weight loss commercials and so many others. The different companies advertise their programs and promise results. Well, they all work if you work them. The point is, how willing is anyone to do the work?

The commercial ends and the news goes on and on about opioid addiction. Prescription pain pills are a huge problem. This is an epidemic and a public health crisis. Overdosing has become a routine nightmare. One young man wrote in a note to his mother before he died of an overdose, "At first it was fun and then it became a full-time job."

I keep remembering the image of you on TV at the dinner for your inauguration. I noticed that when a congratulatory toast was offered, you raised your glass, but did not drink. You put the glass down. Good for you. I am sorry that your brother died from the horror of alcoholism.

We are all fighting one addiction or another. We are anxious and pop pills to calm down. We are depressed and pop pills to cheer up. I remember chuckling when former President Obama admitted he was trying to quit smoking. He admitted that when he was a young man, he was caught up with smoking weed. Or is it pot? What is marijuana called these days?

You, my President, have not been an angel. I forgive you. I forgive all of us. I want to get to the core of this mass mania. Are we spiritually bankrupt? Do we need a great awakening? In the sixties, I thought we were making love, not war. I remember hosting "love-ins" behind my carriage house in Sea Cliff on Long Island. All the top rock stars came and hung out as my husband was the lead singer in a band. We wrote songs together. One was called, *Jesus Saves the Poor*and nobody wanted to record it. The recording companies thought the name "Jesus" was too provocative.

Get this. Hillary wants her own TV show. Lord knows she can afford to produce one. Great idea. I wonder if she will be able to pull off being likable like Oprah or Ellen? I would watch it. Point, counter point! I bounce from CNN to FOX NEWS all day long. Hillary, we all want our own television show. Well, join the club, get in line. At last, you are one of us.

I'M BACK

_____

February 10, 2017

Dear Donald,

    I sold my magazine to a really bright young woman who is teaching at Kent State University. We have a five year payout arrangement. I am retaining a small interest plus working with her to get her running and strong. The magazine reaches close to one hundred thousand women in three Ohio counties. It is a marvelous endeavor. Oprah copied me. I swear she did. My TV show on Long Island was running long before her Sunday show. It was so much like what she does now. Our magazines have a similar soul. Who am I kidding? Oprah is amazing. I loved the article she has in the current O magazine. She gathered a bunch of women who were staunch Republicans and Democrats, and got them to talk to each other all day. This was to communicate, not compete; to share and not shun; to empower, not demoralize.

    I believe that the problem in government is money and power. Everyone is holding onto their jobs. Some days, I think that the American dream has backfired and the system of government cannot work. Other days, I am so overwhelmed with sentiment and gratitude for the fact that I was born in this amazing country.

Even though I haven't written in a while, I have been watching closely what you are doing. I would like to be Press Secretary. It looks like the most exciting and interesting job. Then again, I shudder at the thought of taking on all of that rancor and dissent. Is your staff normal? How to they shoulder all of this? How does Kelly Ann do what she does along with managing a family and four children? How does Ivanka deal with endless confusion and criticism? How does your marriage survive this heartless scrutiny?

Michele Obama can't get enough. Now she wants a TV show! Everyone wants to be on television. Some say that television is a thing of the past, not so. The White House Press Secretary, because of television, is getting more attention than the soap operas and talk shows.

This administration, for better or worse, is the most intriguing and entertaining ever. What a reality show it is! I have to stay tuned all day to keep up! I don't want to miss any twist or turn in the plot. I am not just participating vicariously, I am America! I am moving my agenda forward in step with what is going on in the world. I am passionate in doing all that I can to make a difference. I am asking, "What can my country do for me?" And, "What can I do for my country?" I am going to give and I am going to get. There is nothing wrong with that plan.

GOLF ANYONE?

February 11, 2017

Dear Donald,

How relaxing to imagine you playing golf with Shinzo Abe, the Prime Minister of Japan. He is also the grandson of the former PM of Japan, Nobusuke Kishi who played golf with President Eisenhower. I hear Shinzo Abe is visiting you at Mar-A-Lago in Florida and has presented you with a golden golf club. What fun! And there is a dinner party tonight. Oh, how I wish that I could be there. I envy the flurry of excitement as droves of staff set up the social and business events related to this very important week.

The Prime Minister of Japan seems to be reaching out to you. The Chinese are pushing you a bit even though you are supporting the "One China Policy." Our relationship with Beijing and East Asia is a little testy. You keep digging big political holes and I keep holding my breath, hoping that you can dig out.

"Please be careful" and "please don't be so careful" are wishes that confuse me daily. This endless political correctness across the globe is exhausting. You let us all breathe. And you are a breath of fresh air. But, at the same time, we all know that some restraint is wise. I am rooting for you and I believe in you. But, at the same time, I am cringing and ducking. Slow down a bit. Think carefully. Like I know anything. I am not alone in these thoughts. A lot of your supporters are holding their breath. You are bold and brave and so over the top, that we are aghast. I would like to relax and know we are all in good hands. Maybe I should go out to play a round of golf.

I have a condo on a golf course in St. Petersburg Beach. It is gorgeous. I forced myself to learn to golf and to wear the golf attire that did not flatter my figure. I was a member of a wonderful country club on Long Island where Rudy Giuliani often golfed. Did you golf with him? Maybe you did. I think you did. I hope you didn't see me huffing and puffing, missing shots and longing for the first nine holes to be over. I looked forward to sitting luxuriously at lunch in the clubhouse with a mimosa. Oh, please don't be angry with me, I am not a drinker. Really, I am not. But after these endless games of golf, I just wanted an escape.

You must know that I was the kind of kid who couldn't climb the rope in gym class. But I learned to sail, and loved it. I learned to ski and there were moments of great joy. There were also moments I couldn't wait to get to the lodge. I learned to swim, but never competitively. I could dive too, but why? I loved ice skating which is my kind of sport. There were the pretty skates, great outfits, smooth gliding, lots of fun with friends, the exhilaration of winter air, piped in music and the hot chocolate breaks. Heaven. Golf? Not so much.

My home in Ohio is on a golf course. I have lived here for fourteen years and have not golfed once. I have been so busy with my magazine. You can run a dynasty and a country and still have time to golf. It amazes me. Okay Donald, this spring I am going to golf again. If you can find time to do it, so can I. And maybe one day, we'll go to a driving range and you can give me a few pointers.

ARMS

————————

Dear Donald,

Today, I confidently walked into church late. I even went to the front row to sit in my usual seat next to my black friend, Marlene. I mention she is black because my church community is very diverse racially, culturally, politically, and in every other way. We get along very well. I am proud and grateful for that. Our congregation is a model of reconciliation for our country.

It took every effort to straighten out my payroll this morning. To figure out who gets what and what is left over and how much to pay clients sometimes takes all of my energy. I am working on my magazine harder than ever now that I have sold it. It is complicated. Television is much easier than this. The details are flooding my brain and there are so many people and situations to navigate. Money is involved in each relationship so I cannot afford mistakes. How do you do it?

The Grammy Awards are on tonight. I am not looking forward to watching as I cannot bear all of the negative political

————————

comments. I could mention that you set the tone. You were brutal in the campaign and the backlash is upsetting. I know you had to do what you did to win. You had to fight mercilessly. You said what a lot of people were thinking. But now it is time to get off of this negative spiral and work together for the common good. It is your turn to govern and it should be with the respect of the citizens, all of us, for you or at least, the office.

Church does this to me. I wince at harsh statements and long for a soothing, passionate, peaceful and rational world. You are a new creature with a thousand arms and you have the ability to use them all to solve a thousand issues. I will watch and learn and ask God to give me more ability to make the world a better place. And when I find a mountain too high to climb, I will say, "Be thou removed."

VALENTINE

———

February 15, 2017

Dear Donald,

Don't think for a minute that I forgot about you on Valentine's Day. It was a busy day for me. I bought a new Apple 7 iPhone and had to go back and forth to the store four times to ask questions. Then, I went to DSW to buy a pair of sensational suede boots with high, thin heels.

I am trying to put together an outfit for a huge event coming up next month. I am going to receive an award for making a difference in the lives of women. I am glad to receive this. I have a love/hate relationship with you. I admire you so much and I am inspired to keep pushing for more accomplishments and self-expression.

Yesterday, I had the most enchanting Valentine's Day. Dale and I enjoyed a romantic dinner. Dale surprised me with a gift bag full of carefully chosen treats, a beautiful bottle of my favorite perfume, chocolate strawberries, a romantic card and a little stuffed dog that I named "Valentine." I carry that little dog

35

everywhere. When he is perched on the top of my purse, I talk to him like Tom Hanks talked to the basketball in the movie, *Castaway.*

Some days I feel stranded on an island as the political parties are so contentious and far apart in their views. The rancor is making me ill. I was up in the middle of the night, sick to my stomach. When I had lunch with my cousin, Diane, I discovered that she also had the same physical response to all of this political upheaval. My friend who is a Democrat, is also physically ill over politics. How did we all drift so far apart? My friend who did not vote for you no longer speaks to me. This is really disturbing.

One of my friends claims she doesn't watch the news or read newspapers. She feels so much of it is contrived cheap sensationalism. I first thought she was mad, or at least strange, because of her approach to contemporary life. Who is the crazy one here? The one who avoids or the one who is addicted?

I am determined to rationally and calmly sort it all out. In a few weeks I am going with Diane to visit her sister in Florida. Maybe we will stop at Mar-a-Lago to see you. We are obsessed with your administration and are cheering for you! Our Valentine gift to you is that the three of us have agreed to pray for you as you take on the world.

RAINBOW

February 16, 2017

Dear Donald,

We live in beautiful and exciting times! The other day, it was gray and snowy and not a very pretty day at all. Suddenly, a rainbow appeared in the winter sky! Today, evidence of King Tut's tomb was discovered. The market is 20,620! What on earth? Whoever expected the market to go up so high? Mike Flynn resigned at your request, but I know there is a part of you that is not happy about it. I am heartbroken. This has been a controversial administration, but the accomplishments are amazing. There are so many jobs being created. Things went well at the meeting with world leaders of Israel, Britain and Japan.

My son has been saving to buy a home on Long Island. The housing market there is "over the moon"! Prices are high and taxes are high. I am thrilled that after looking, he found a wonderful house on the market in his price range. I have a prayer chain organized and praying that he gets this house.

I have a prayer chain organized for you too, Donald. The

negativity has been overwhelming from the beginning of the campaign, all the way to weeks after the inauguration. Neil Cavuto of FOX NEWS asked commentators today if they could at least cover some positive things? The political left complains that you are not dignified. I love dignified. But I have seen a lot of smoother operators who are "dripping" with class and diplomacy. They are articulate and thoughtful but have not moved our country in a direction that made me happy or hopeful.

Dr. Sabastian Gorka, is convinced that there is no unbiased coverage of this president. He believes that reported stories bear no resemblance to what he witnessed when he was in the room where they took place. Gorka says, "The media is pouncing on the negative and refusing to focus on anything at all that is working." You, Donald, refuse to tell anyone what you are going to do. Strategy is about surprise. In that way, I am not like you.

I am extremely diplomatic, but maybe that is fine. I cannot be you and yet, I want to learn from you. What I am learning most is to work relentlessly and to be impervious to my fear. I am mastering fear. There is no hope of accomplishing my mission if I let fear paralyze me. At times, fear stops me from sending an email or an invoice to a client. I need to see myself as a winner, as you see yourself. This is what intrigues me the most. You believe in yourself and so I believe in you. You are bringing back coal and confidence and rainbows when we least expect them.

SUNNY DAYS

Dear Donald,

It is sunny here in Cleveland, Ohio today. This is the first time ever, that we hit a temperature over 62 degrees in February and the sky is blue, blue, blue! You are in sunny Florida holding a rally for your political base. They are very excited to see you. Thousands of fans have been lining up for hours to show support. I know you are going to enjoy this because a lot of the county has opposed you at every turn.

It is Saturday and I am relentlessly pushing myself to accomplish my goals. I am pacing myself, as the purpose is not be become exhausted but to be consistent, measured and committed to advancing. After I finish my "to do" list, my inclination is to leave my desk and put things off until later, or tomorrow. I stop and ask myself the following question: "Sandra, are you really in need of a break now? Or, can you work a little longer and get more things accomplished?" The least of which is writing a page to you.

I remember the first time Nancy Pelosi was named the head of

---

the Democratic Party. I was so excited to see a woman in such a powerful position. Today, I am not so proud of her and I don't often agree with her thinking.

Norma McCorvey, aka "Jane Roe" of abortion rights fame (Roe v. Wade), died today. She was 69 and lived in an assisted-living facility. That is not very old. She deeply regretted her involvement in the Roe v. Wade decision and actively campaigned for pro-life as she matured. I can relate to that.

Nancy Pelosi and Hillary Clinton are women I now see from a different perspective as I have aged. I deeply regret the many times I expressed support for Roe v. Wade to my students when the law was first passed. As young women, we didn't know about prenatal technology and research. While I am not making excuses for myself, I think that many women, with more awareness, are heartbroken regarding their young decisions to abort their children. This extends to their careless decisions to engage in unprotected sex or even sexual intimacy outside of marriage. I grew up in the "make love, not war" era. What I didn't see, was the utter brutality of our decisions to engage in sexual activities. The devil will show you a darned good time, but the devil is a liar. In time, after luring you, he will turn on you and destroy you.

Oma Abdel Rahman also died today. He was in prison for 9/11 terrorist attacks and was the master mind behind so much terrorism. He thought he was doing something noble and right. Did he, like Jane Roe and I, regret his thinking or violent acts? Was he concerned about meeting his "Maker" or feel a need to repent?

I grieve when I think about the hundreds of millions of men, women and children, born and unborn, who were killed over the centuries by wars and other means. Will this ever change? Maybe someday there will be peace on earth. We will have found a way to stop killing each other and ourselves. That has never happened before. But, then again, Cleveland never had spring weather in February, until today.

WINGS OF AN EAGLE

March 19, 2017

Dear Donald,

I spoke in church today, about tithing. I usually do that at the beginning of each month because I practice this discipline. It still scares me even though I have been doing it for a while. I don't understand how I am keeping up with my expenses. I seem to have the bills paid and I am feeling richer than ever. I think that feeling rich is a state of mind rather than a bank balance. There are many ways to feel rich.

I do not object to having some disposable income and being financially secure. However, my spiritual wealth is my greatest treasure. I would love to have gold and silver overflowing in my bank accounts. But God keeps showing me other blessings such as music, laughter, companionship, family fun, sunshine, great food and permission to take some time off.

I had a glorious five days in Florida with my cousins. We enjoyed great weather, poolside laughter, shopping, dining and stepping out to comedy and night club acts. Together, at my cousin's house, we watched award winning films and filled our bellies with junk food and soda as we learned more about each other. Like some families, we have experienced some tension through the years. I was able to end that through my connection to Spirit. This gathering was filled with only love, acceptance and joy.

In the last few weeks, I have been honored with an international award for being an "alpha" woman. The award was given by the organization, Elite Women Around the World. I have a golden statue on my mantelpiece. While I am proud, of it, I don't feel that I really deserve it. I am growing into it and allowing myself to feel worthy. I believe my success in all that I do is attributed to God. When I honor God, God honors me.

I just learned that your 2005 tax returns were released against your wishes. You paid more money in taxes that one year than I have earned in a lifetime! I heard you don't give to charity. I don't see you that way at all. I see you as a very charitable man, in many ways. I worry about your faults and vulnerabilities as I do my own. I pray for you and for myself, for my family, world governments, poverty and how to end it. The list goes on and on. We don't have to worry, with enough prayer and praise, according to the Old Testament prophet Isaiah, "They shall mount up with wings as eagles."

PAIN

March 27, 2017

Dear Donald,

The war in Iraq is escalating and the stock market is down nine days in a row. The DOW is still very high, but it has dropped a little bit each of the last nine days. The hostility between the Democrats and Republicans is demoralizing. The "head banging" among the establishment Republicans is discouraging and infuriating. You, and everyone who supported you, thought you could wave your magic wand of business experience and heal the planet. But the world keeps spinning and there is still climate change, scientific and political. Some don't want healing of any sort as long as you are in office.

I don't know what to do. Food is a pacifier for me. I would love some macaroni and cheese, a bowl of cereal and a cup of hot tea with honey from Ohio bees. I am sure you know that bees are in trouble. If they disappear we will have to hand pollinate and that doesn't seem sustainable. Is that from climate change or chemicals?

It feels grim. The news is not good. With all of the opinions and slams heard on the news stations, one would think the world is coming to an end. Tax reform is the subject of the moment and, of course, the reports are negative.

Everyone I know is all over the social media and it is making us more social but less intimate. People are more lonely than ever. Families are scattered across the country and some across the globe. FaceTime and Facebook are the only means of contact and it is unsatisfying. Those connections, although better than nothing, leave people still craving physical contact like a hug or a kiss. We are stuck to our computers and phones, all of us, teens and adults. I check Facebook for pictures and posts from my grandchildren and daughter-in-law. That is the light in all of the darkness of the day.

Today, with all of the good you do, your popularity wanes, but stay strong and be of good cheer. I remember the polls before you were elected! It is sad that you took on more problems and you are having difficulty getting support for the solutions. Remember, "The sun will come up tomorrow...it's only a day away."

PUSHING

March 28, 2017

Dear Donald,

Today you were so nice to the coal miners. They were standing on the stage dressed very casually. You wore your red tie. You always look presidential! Rick Perry was decked out looking very slick in some ways, but down to earth in others. He was in a setting of what I would call "regular guys." Even the miner executives looked "home town." You are not like anyone else who has held the highest office of our land. You look ready to roll up you sleeves and solve problems.

The night of your speech to congress, you were smooth and dignified. I was so happy to see it. Everyone wants you to be like that all of the time. I am not sure that I do. I like that part of you who grew up working next to your dad on construction sites. I can relate to that. It is real and makes sense. You worked brick by brick, board by board, building a wall, a country and a legacy.

Each day is another intense schedule as I work with my new publisher to get the magazine out. In addition, I write my books, handle my homes in Ohio and Florida, speak at church, lead groups and nurture my relationships, not the least of which is my large Lebanese family. Are there enough hours in a day?

I am pushing. The word "pushing" brings to mind the hard work, pain and determination. I need to give birth to my projects. And once born, there are years of nurturing those projects required to insure success. You are the power of example. I watch your tireless pushing and I am inspired to keep up with you and to continue to give birth to my dreams.

TAKE IT ON

April 3, 2017

Dear Donald,

Tell me, do you have days when you just don't want to be President of the United States? Or, at least you don't want to confront the issues on your desk? You always look like you can't wait to conquer the next problem or challenge. You act like you're winning even when the facts stack up against you and it looks like a loss may be pending. Today, I don't want to be president, that's for sure. I don't want to fight the fraud that I suspect with a transaction I engaged in a number of years ago. My attorney has to look at the notes. It may be that I have a case, but waited too long to prosecute.

For me, the problem with being a "good" Christian is that I can't make anybody wrong, even if they are wrong. I keep forgiving and forgetting. I know, my thinking is convoluted. I need to confront evil, Donald, but you have no idea how much I hate confrontation. You, on the other hand, seem to thrive on it. Your opposition can't throw enough insults. You stand up to it, not smoothly or diplomatically, but quickly and emphatically. Who intimidates you? The Democrats? The hostile press? The North Koreans?

You are the lion who has courage. I am the lion who needs to be "off to see the Wizard" in the famous movie, *The Wizard of Oz!* I am so concerned with being lady-like, soft spoken, trusting and friendly. I had such a caring and protective father that I cannot imagine genuine malice and incessant thieves. By the time I work up enough steam to go after the bad guy, the culprit has left the country, died or disappeared. Then the law states: "Sorry, you are just a little too late to complain about this!" I guess it's only stealing if you catch them early. Who made up that rule?

Stamina and grit. I know I need that and I am working at it. Really, I am. Robert Nardelli, former Chrysler and Home Depot CEO, says you are facing tremendous adversity, but he has faith in you. How do you fight and fight and fight and still look like you're having a good time? Don't let the presidency age you. Let's both stand up against the wear and tear of ugly, exasperating opposition! I'll breathe in your relentless winning spirit and we'll take on life itself.

BITTERSWEET

———————

April 6, 2017

Dear Donald,

The children are gasping for air. Babies are foaming at the mouth and dying. A very young man, the same age as my precious grandson, is filmed in Syria as he sobs in a state of shock and grief. He lost 19 family members from a lethal chemical weapons attack. According to news reports, in seven years, over half of a million Syrian citizens have died at the hands of Assad. You are moved, shocked and determined to do something about it. Enough. You have had enough, Donald. You are not alone, we have all had enough. On both sides of the aisle, at the UN and across the globe, so many of us have had enough. We do not want war, but we do want to put a stop to this.

My life goes on through it all. I watched this horrendous news coverage about Syria on my iPhone while I was getting my hair done at my favorite salon. I had a "mani-pedi" in the morning and there were so many shades of pink from which to choose, it was difficult to make a decision. My manicurist was puzzled at my indecisiveness.

Why was I in such a fog? I live, walk and eat in health, I have reasonable wealth and often walk in peace and pleasure. I drive to opulent appointments by way of picturesque winding roads and wind up at shops where friends greet me with hugs and tea. I try to celebrate life and enjoy it but today, I cannot decide on a nail polish color.

In my mind's eye, I see the image of the crying child who lost his family. I just can't let go of it partially because the news stations play it over and over again. And because I have a kind and gentle heart, I am spending my energy pushing the fear, sadness and horror away so that I don't have to internalize it quite as much.

Death is all around. On Saturday, I will attend a wake and comfort my friend who is burying his very old mother. She lived a long life and my friend was kind and attentive to her. I try to cancel my thoughts of the pictures of the horror in Syria. A father holding his dead infant son next to his dead wife said he was glad his loved ones were in heaven and did not have to live in Syria. My dad was born in Syria. I heard stories of a beautiful country. What happened?

Will you be golfing with the head of China this weekend? In spite of all that happens around the world? Are you like me, overcome with gratitude for a beautiful life? And do you shudder at the horror of injustice everywhere and are you sad that there may not be a peaceful solution?

ARAB SPRING

April 7, 2017

Dear Donald,

This is scary! I totally get how upset you are about the chemical weapons that were used in Syria against Assad's people, including helpless little children. I was heartbroken to see the human devastation. The whole world seems upset. Russia is sending a war ship into the Black Sea. Assad swears he did nothing wrong, that he did not use chemical weapons. Some members of Congress felt you should have debated with them before sending the missiles. Of course, they are all on spring vacations. Some spring! It snowed in Cleveland today. No kidding, six inches of heavy snow fell and is confusing the blossoming trees. Arab spring has also been very, very cold.

I braved the snow and chaired a meeting at the senior center. I got there an hour early, as I always do, to prepare the room for the session. Then I read the chapter that we would be discussing. Recovery deals with "nervous" people. Some of them have received considerable treatments for their high anxiety.

Donald, I am a "get better" junkie. Believe me, I am all better, about as better as a person can be! I have attended every get better group, study, church program, book club and society ever known. I did lay therapy in New York. Because of my experiences, I believe I knew more than the therapists, no kidding.

But Donald, really, what is going on is enough to create a lot of anxiety in all of us. Syria, Russia, Iran, China and North Korea all at the same time! This is way too much for the average nervous girl, much less the really sensitive girls, like me. The other day, my cousin Diane recommended a bag of caramel and cheese popcorn to soothe my soul. I foolishly purchased the supersized bag. More than half of it is gone. I munch my way through the tension I feel over today's news.

I am worrying about everything. I am concerned about Melania's fashion choices. She is gorgeous, but I don't think she should wear low necklines or sleeveless dresses. Okay, I concede that I am being a bit extreme, but the wives of the other leaders around the world seem to be more covered up. I suppose if they looked like Melania, they might dress differently. I am not sure of that. Melania is lovely and sweet, but I am concerned. Being so beautiful can provoke others. Donald, she is doing really great. Forget I ever said anything. Don't tell her. Her dresses are only slightly glamorous and she can't walk around in a sack just to quiet the damsels in distress.

Melania adores her son and you adore all of your children. As parents, you are impeccable. Because you are a great dad, it does not surprise me that your red line was drawn when it came to the abuse and cruelty to the children in Syria. I want to protect your wife because other women can be so cruel. She can't do anything about her looks. She should be admired by all of us. I fear that women will punish her for being an immigrant, the first lady and for her beauty. I am sane enough to know just how crazy we all are.

LETTERS

April 9, 2017

Dear Donald,

I don't know why I started writing letters to you, but it is very important to me. Kenneth Copeland recently wrote about the letters he writes to his prayer partners. Do you know Kenneth Copeland? I love his preaching about healing. Trust me, it works. I have recovered from some serious health issues using the guidance he offers, leaning on the scriptures he suggested. He said, "Ever since the Church began, letters have been a powerful tool in God's hand. God entrusted the gospel message to be communicated by letters. These letters attributed to Paul, John, Luke and others carried powerful messages to God's people. They did in ancient times and still do today."

I have never felt so involved in world affairs. And I care so deeply about the suffering of so many around the globe. I am riveted to all of the news about international events and I have acquired a deep respect for those who govern. I am frustrated because so often, the endless debate and disagreement sabotages any real progress. Despite all that is wrong and corrupt, I still have a feeling of hope in my heart.

My friends Gale and Will are staunch Democrats. They are African-Americans and huge supporters of everything Barack Obama did and will ever do. Dale and I leaned in a Republican direction this past election. When the four of us get together, we rant and rave and debate. We try to keep open minds and hearts. We will love each other in spite of our political polarities. In fact, they have brought us closer together. I grow listening to them and I hope that they grow listening to us. Listening to understand is essential.

I invited Gale and Will to the awards ceremony where I was honored. They are proud of me and genuinely support me. Gale and Will are detectives and are very self-confident. When I first met Gale, over ten years ago, I felt known, appreciated and respected. She was never threatened by my successes or competitive. She is free enough in her soul to give me an endless standing ovation. Gale gets the same from me. I took her out to a tea house for her birthday and she dressed like the queen she is. She is a queen of a Red Hat Society chapter. On this occasion, she wore blue from head to toe, from hat to heels. She is stunning. I am glad to be associated with her.

ONE HUNDRED DAYS

April 29, 2017

Dear Donald,

It is almost May and everyone is talking about your first 100 days. Yesterday, I watched you speak in Harrisburg, Pennsylvania to around eleven thousand people. I understand your frustration and I hesitate to ever make you wrong because you have demonstrated a unique ability to win. You get what you want. And you articulate a very clear plan for our country. However, I am sad about the relationship between you and the press. I didn't like that you did not attend the dinner in Washington that celebrated the media. You were thrilled at not attending the Washington Correspondence Dinner. Please, can you find a way to build a bridge to the press which is not in flames?

I agree with you regarding the negativity of the media, but I think it is time to consider some reconciliation. This constant argument is painful for all of us and living through it day after day is agonizing. I wish the press would support you and moderate its tone, be respectful and encouraging and report actual news and

---

not opinions and "what if" scenarios. I want you to be larger than the conflict.

Is there some space between Obama's careful and sometimes ineffective political correctness and your sometimes accusatory manner? I was frustrated by Obama's apologies and drawling patient explanations. At times I am shocked by your fury, disrespect and lack of diplomacy.

I am tired today. After a glorious few weeks with family and grandchildren, I am overspent emotionally and financially. A mild winter left me and Dale with a springtime full of staggering allergies. Dale was in bed with something that kept him out of work for four days. He never misses work. Do you ever get sick? What is your secret to your strength and stubborn resolve? I feel like I am caving this week. Your intense energy, more often than not, inspires me.

Today, I feel a bit insignificant. I have made a bargain with myself. Every time I make a positive and productive step, I give myself one hundred blessings. Every time I pass up a cookie, work on a project, reach out to a friend or embrace a positive attitude, I pour out those blessings. Do you remember Dr. Norman Vincent Peale and the *Power of Positive Thinking*? We both loved that book and you never forget it. You plow through it demanding results while I try to catch up.

There are so many positive and powerful people who are so inspiring to me. For that I am grateful.

PLANET IN RETROGRADE

May 1, 2017

Dear Donald,

I woke up this morning not wanting to face the day. Doing anything productive was just beyond me. My wonderful doctor friend, Stuart, prescribed an antibiotic and strong cough syrup for me. It really worked! I should have consulted him sooner. Even with the help of super medications, I was tired, foggy and dragging myself to get my morning coffee. I pushed myself to get things done and every task was a struggle. If I were an astrologist, I would tell you that it feels that Mercury is in retrograde. I emailed my astrologist and told her that my life seems to be unraveling. She told me to let it happen for a while and then the optical illusion will pass. Sanity will return. My day was an uphill battle of my computer breaking down to unpaid bill notices that were already paid.

I noticed that Ebony is now hosting *The Five* on FOX NEWS. She is beautiful and wearing my signature color, fuchsia. Her hair is perfect. She is young. I know I am not as young as I used to be, but lots of people haven't figured that out yet. I am relentless in my efforts to fight the aging process. Along with Ebony, Joe Namath, of all people, is also hosting on *The Five* today. Really? What can he know? He is a relic. I guess he is fighting to stay relevant too.

Why can't you get that kid out of North Korea? And why can't I be rich and famous? I miss my grandchildren and I am considering paying for a Disney cruise. It will not be an easy task for me. I will have to work hard and carefully save. You could buy the ship! This is part of my love/hate relationship with you. I am thrilled by your success and you are grabbing rainbows by the fistful. The correspondents lining up to interview you are swelling with pride and excitement. At the same time, they are lusting for what you have. The money, fame, excitement, world influence, and a happy and successful loving family. Let's not forget the Trump Tower and The White House.

Either Mercury is in retrograde or I am losing my focus. It is not how high I can climb that matters. What matters is the thrill of the climb. The joy is in the relentless willingness to play the game of life as long and hard as I can. There is always a way to keep playing. Find the way and fall in love with it. I have to stop trying to catch up to you and just be happy with me.

HEALTHCARE

_____

May 3, 2017

Dear Donald,

Tomorrow, the House of Representatives votes again for the repeal and replacement of Obamacare. What does this mean? I listened and I am still confused. I don't want anyone to suffer and I think people who abuse their health need to take some responsibility for that. But who doesn't abuse their health in one way or another? It is really difficult to sort all of that out. I suppose that drug and alcohol abuse, extreme overweight and smoking might be considered. Governing and voting are so complicated. To be a responsible voter is exhausting. I consider the pros and cons of issues every day.

Dale received news today that someone he knew was killed in a motorcycle accident. He was only fifty-four and had a son in his twenties who wanted to find him and reconnect. He is too late. Dale and I often talk about how sad it is to see a family fall apart. With our first marriages, we knew there was more we could have done to try to make things work. We see our own mistakes as well

_____

as the mistakes of our ex-spouses. But what does this have to do with healthcare? Couples counseling might have helped.

Comey was on TV rehashing the Hillary Clinton investigation. Very emotional issues all day long. There is still the news of Russia, North Korea, Syria and on and on. With all of the horrors of the world and confusion in our country, I worked calmly at my desk, getting coffee at Dunkin' Donuts, doing banking and getting my hair done.

While eating Chinese food for dinner, I learned that a North Korean girl wrote a book about her escape from her homeland. It was a nightmare of death and horror. She looked like a little movie star when she was interviewed on TV. Reality has become surreal. If I were Amish, would I know of any of this? They have plenty of drama of their own.

For me, right now, healthcare is turning off the television and focusing on a quiet and loving evening. I can do that. I can't do much about the rest.

FBI - COMEY

May 11, 2017

Dear Donald,

Thank heavens for Congressman Peter King. He made you sound like you made the correct decision to fire Jim Comey. I like Mercedes Schlapp's (White House Director of Strategic Communications) take on the situation. She would have liked you to work with Comey and get him to resign. The dismissal might have been less brutal.

Your team has to be impeccable regarding professionalism and form. McCain's daughter agreed with Schlapp, that there should have been more decorum. Americans agree with you but, my friend, your communications team is letting you down. Slow down and present things in a thoughtful manner.

Will the multibillionaire please stand up? One of the greatest mistakes I have made in life was that I valued those with money more than those without it. Having a huge amount of money like you do, is confusing to the rest of us. How can someone who is so smart, be so careless? Or, are we missing something? We are

---

shocked and stunned by your decisions. But one after another, you lead us in some very positive direction. The sky is not falling. The economy is moving in the right direction. The appointments you have made are pretty remarkable. There is hope for replacing Obamacare with something more workable. The immigration crisis seems to be under better control. The hope of a tax break for all of us is so welcome. I am having a hard time watching the media. So much of it has become toxic, hysterical and dangerously threatening.

I want to start my own television show again. I had one in New York for nine years. I believe that television has the ability to serve as a great healer in our culture. Much of it is doing the opposite. It is violent, insulting and negatively provoking. I would invite the healers. Those who want to use their power, authority and public face to find solutions and bridge building would be my guests. No name calling allowed. Only ideas, encouragement and hope are welcome.

I talked with my sister Shirley, and asked what she thought about all of this? She told me that she doesn't watch TV anymore because it is too upsetting. Shirley looked healthier and prettier than I have seen her in a long time.

Where is the remote? Please, throw it away!

POINT / COUNTERPOINT

———————

May 23, 2017

Dear Donald,

An eight-year-old girl was one of the twenty-two victims of the terror attack at the concert in Manchester, England. I watched it on the news with the rest of the world. While I watched, I tried to concentrate on Christian readings of hope, but I was so tired of it all. Why were backpacks allowed into this venue? Why wasn't there stricter security? Will this ever stop? Exhaustive measures of protection and prevention sweep the globe. The disease of hatred and violence persist.

I couldn't bear the pain of it any longer. My friend was fretting about allowing her teenage daughter to attend a concert at a large venue in Cleveland. What parents would go? How would they get there and get home? Where will they stay after the concert? My friend and her daughter fought all day about the event. The teen wanted the pressure off and the mom was frantic with concern. There were too many loose ends in the planning of the evening.

I looked at the face of the little girl killed in Manchester and at the same time, looked at a picture of my grandson of the same age. I could hardly breathe. The pain of this unspeakable loss for her parents, siblings and friends was unimaginable. The futures of so many were taken.

I was alone watching this horror and had command of the remote. I clicked to a guide to look for something light and hopeful. I decided on the show, *The Bachelor*. The crisis on this channel was that a bachelor wouldn't get a rose, or be rejected, and have to leave the show. One of the bachelors cried when he didn't receive the rose. He had spent a fortune on a wardrobe just to be on television. The one who wore a "penguin suit" was invited to stay by the lovely damsel.

There is a large truck outside with a crew of landscapers mulching all of the yards in my development. The color of the mulch is very important to the residents. It has to be the right shade of brown. I watch as I sip ice water.

This evening, my darling cousin and her husband are joining us to enjoy one of the many concerts on the common in our neighborhood overlooking the pond. She will bring wine with vegetables and dip. It will be good to see my neighbors and experience a departure from this horror to fill my time with peace, music and love.

For now, I am tired and will take a short nap so I will be refreshed for good company and a good evening.

MEMORIAL DAY

May 30, 2017

Dear Donald,

Your opposition and even some who voted for you say that you are gauche. Do they see the beautiful structures you created? The elegant spaces abounding in imagination and grace? "Gauche" is defined as awkward. I see intense certainty and bold determination in you. In your speech today there was nothing but grace and gratitude. I have watched dozens and dozens of such presentations over the years. I cried when you spoke and expressed your genuine and heartfelt sympathies for American families who lost brave and honored soldiers. Your outreach to them was compassionate. You recognized the soldiers who fought for all of us. You fight for us too.

Open borders are awkward and clumsy. Rioting and destroying property is extreme lack of respect for others and their property. Refusing to allow speakers to voice opinions peacefully on college campuses and other venues is tactless and wrong in America.

The knight in shining armor does not have the benefit of film

---

editing. Reels of film are not on the cutting floor. We are watching courage and battle in the raw. You and your followers are not burning down buildings. They are perhaps bold and pushing boundaries, but not without some restraint. Winning in sports, politics and business is sometimes messy. Victory is not always smooth. Winning is passionate, bold and brave. You are all of that.

The ladies in your life smooth out your rough edges. Melania and Ivanka are gracious, grounded and stunning. They glide through space and speak truth as if it is honey and fine wine. They are studied, graceful and present themselves with dignity. On the other hand, you are spontaneous. They are measured. You are a warrior. They are regal ladies of the court. You are tough and they are tender. It is clear to me that you love God. I know that there is a soft and vulnerable side to you. I have seen it. There are many sides to you, none of which are clumsy. You and your staff are ambitious, refining, evolving, bold and determined.

I believe you are, as you are, making America great again!

COMEY CRAZY

———

June 13, 2017

Dear Donald,

I was awake all night. For several days I watched the coverage of the James Comey hearings. I went from station to station to get a well-rounded view. Last night I couldn't sleep. I was deeply upset and concerned about the conflicting coverage. The news is so biased and it is impossible for me to know what to believe. The anger is overwhelming and I am heartsick. I long for a less hostile government. I am doing all that I can to work with my friends of differing political leanings. I make it my mission to listen calmly and to communicate with love and care.

I watched most of the Cavs game and they were winning. I could hardly believe it because the first three games were terrible. I couldn't watch the last quarter for fear that they would lose in the end. I consider myself to be a loyal fan. You have won so much but you haven't won the heart of the nation. Maybe you need LeBron on your team. I pray for you and everyone in government because I believe we all need Divine guidance.

———

I received an award from the Mayor of Cleveland this week and another from a women's group. The awards were for community leadership and for mentoring women. I was so happy to receive them.

I work at seeing myself as someone who has evolved into a good person. It is hard for me to let go of my past mistakes. I know God wants me to see myself as I am today. Like you, I have plenty in my past that would evoke criticism and scorn. Like you, I am fighting to make the world a better place and to bring honor to my family and name. My parents and children deserve the best from me. I am not leaving this earth without giving it to them.

These are intense times. May they manifest into the miraculous.

THREE STRIKES

_____

June 14, 2017

Dear Donald,

It is tragic that only a day or two after I made such a strong statement about the need for Americans, the media and the politicians to calm down their rhetoric, someone took a gun to a baseball field and shot an innocent Republican Congressman while practicing for a charity game. The shooter had a record of being jobless, drunk while driving, being an abuser, short fused and a stubborn neighbor. In addition, he was a threatening spokesperson on social media. I learned he was a Bernie Sanders supporter.

This man was often involved in hate speech. Today, the debates are all about freedom of speech and when it may go too far. Governor Huckabee suggests that we take a walk, listen to some music or go fishing when emotions run hot. Bernie denounced the actions of the shooter who had campaigned for him during the primaries. Nancy Pelosi was outraged for a moment and went along with Speaker Ryan's statement, "If you harm one of us, you harm us all." The bleeding and brutality of hate speech continues to leak, drip by drip, back into the narrative.

Huckabee calls the *New York Times* "diseased organs" and Sarah Palin threatens to sue them over the retracted accusation that she had something to do with the Gabby Gifford shooting. Even Ebony on *The Five*on FOX NEWS believed that the NYT should apologize to Sarah.Ted Nugent, in essence, said we need to talk nice.

We all need to step back. The media is empowered to lift up the hearts, minds and spirits of their audiences. It used to be that way. Television was more wholesome when Perry Como and his peers were around. Was all of that programming untrue?

It was a nicer, more innocent world when I was growing up. Television was new, clean, entertaining and informative. Now, the news and even regular programming has to be filtered through the squint of my eyes. The violence, hate and immorality have taken over the programming and commercial cinema. Is all of this negativity impacting our emotions and moods? Could it be blamed for all of the depression and violence in our society? Is it part of a bigger plan to break down the morale of Americans? All of that bombardment on our brains that is not clean, pure or chaste can't be good for us. Laughter is good. Love is good. Community is good. I don't see much of that on television.

I think that we all need to detach and go on a media fast. It would give our minds the space to reinvent our values and look at our own quiet and decent lives. We are rushing from one thing to the next. We may be doing good things like driving kids, walking the dogs, going to work, visiting family and getting involved in charitable activities. But still at stop lights, we are checking text messages and emails. Television programming depicts us as a nation of neurotics. Most of us in my generation are pretty basic. We are busy cleaning the house, getting supper on the table and supporting American values. I hope we don't "hate speech" our way out of the American dream.

SMILING

June 27, 2017

Dear Donald,

I have good news! I registered for a special workshop that will last for ten weeks. It is designed to help me finish the draft of my book, *Dear Donald.* The workshop demands a lot of rigorous attention and intention to write and finish the first draft. I am excited about making that happen.

Then, there is more good news. Salem Radio, a nationally syndicated station, invited me to air my radio program. This will be my opportunity to spread love to the nation. Someday, I will interview you, Melania, Ivanka and the rest of your children. Just wait, you will see.

Today, I met with a women's group and we prayed for our country. Among the women there was so much hope and optimism. I am reminded that when I am in the right frame of mind I can walk on hot coals in my bare feet and not get burned. I have done that.

God bless you, Donald! How do you do this work? Melania has

---

to be exhausted too. Both of you are smiling this week. Is it real? Are you happy? You both have fond memories of Saudi Arabia, Israel and the Pope. Dignitaries from around the world continue to visit the White House as well, and they all look so happy to see you! Melania, you are wearing pink and designers are flocking to dress the first lady. You are both winning a lot of things.

The Supreme Court supported your travel restrictions. Now, the health care plan haunts you. I love the way you are dealing and looking for a way to make a good plan for all of America. The economy is hopeful. Do you two sometimes wonder how you ended up in the White House, of all places? My guess is you have both mastered walking on hot coals in your bare feet.

THE SALT

July 2, 2017

Dear Donald,

In two days, it will be Independence Day. Tomorrow, Dale and I are going to my nephew's home to celebrate the 80th and 75th birthdays of two of my cousins. About one hundred people will be there. They have a lot of friends and family. My cousins have served the church for many years doing visitations. They are always at the bedside of people in the hospital or who are ill or will have surgery.

My cousins are invited to a lot of special occasions because people love them. It is reciprocal. Their children fawn over them because they are loving and devoted parents and grandparents. They live in a modest home that is welcoming to all who visit them. At Christmas, they offer gifts of prayers, holy oil, baked goods and pickled turnips. They call around the country just to sing *Happy Birthday!* They offer their kindness and hospitality to the masses. These people voted for you. Deplorable? Hardly! They have had many sleepless nights worrying about the stress you are under. They pray for you.

I think these people have perfect hearts, at least as a human heart can be. They believe in you. I hope you are honored by this. I am sure their prayers go right to the throne of Heaven. I think they have a direct line.

My cousin, Diane, is more spiritually "tuned in" than the rest of us. I have never experienced her being anything other than wise and kind. You have good souls on your side. I must say that my cousins also root for the Cavaliers and Cleveland Indians who just won 12 games in a row. Do you think they're cheering for these teams had anything to do with the victories?

My prayer today is that my cousins continue to live long and meaningful lives. They are treasures to all who know them. I think they are a couple of stars from the heavens and light up our earth. They are a reminder that there is hope for humanity. They are our cheerleaders. Aren't we blessed?

VOLARE! SCARAMUCCI

July 21, 2017

Dear Donald,

I find myself humming that old Italian song, "Volare" as I watch the new White House Communications Director, Anthony Scaramucci. Oh, I love Italians. I married one. Mediterranean cultures can be so warm, lush and romantic. I was used to Lebanese hospitality and soon learned that Italian hospitality was equally inviting. The many years of my marriage were filled with incredible ethnic cooking. My mother-in-law's "red gravy" and meatballs were a culinary delight that equaled no other I had ever experienced.

Mr. Scaramucci repeated a number of times, "I love the president." He defended all of the ideas of your administration and also you! Scaramucci was calm, powerful and controlled while being gracious and not intimidating. He was not elegant and stiff but approachable. He was finely dressed, more out of respect for you than a need to impress. He didn't wear "Harvard" on his sleeve. He conveys a persona of being in charge.

Chris Wallace observed that Scaramucci talks like a New York "street guy." He has made a ton of money and he exuded confidence. His friend is Jay Seculow, your supporter and Republican legal counselor. I deeply respect Seculow. I wonder if I ran into Scaramucci at church back in the day when I lived in New York. He looks like he is that kind of guy. Where there is holy water, blessings can't be far behind.

EMERGENCY FOOD

July 22, 2017

Dear Donald,

There is advertising for emergency food packages that are preserved in such a way, that with proper storage, they will stay fresh and edible for twenty-five years! Maybe we need to freeze-dry or specially pack our pills and potions too. Joseph in the Bible stored food to protect his people when a famine was predicted. The Mormons have always been "preppers" storing food in case of disaster. They keep enough for themselves and for the neighbors.

It started on Christian television broadcasting and it has now found an audience on other channels. A happy family is pictured sitting around a dinner table, in the dark, enjoying their vacuum packed or freeze dried food. It is amazing to me that food can be stored for such a long time. I hate to admit that I am going to pay closer attention.

When I was growing up, my friend Melanie used to come to my house in the morning. My father would drive us to school.

Melanie's dad built a bomb shelter in their basement and stocked it with canned food, bottled water, medicines, first aid supplies and other survival items. He had also packed tents, flashlights, hammers, nails and who knows what else. I thought it was crazy. Today, decades later, the narrative around the bomb shelter mentality is growing.

At school, we were taught to be terrified of the Russians and frequently had bomb drills and took shelter under our desks. Every US citizen was informed about "duck and cover" for protection against a nuclear attack. I never took it seriously. Would it really help? Schools were tagged with a radiation symbol and were deemed as "fallout shelters." I don't know if they really were effective against nuclear radiation or if they just made people feel better. Dale, my companion, reminds me to lock car doors, house doors and windows. He warns me to keep quiet about myself. He says, "They don't need to know that much about you." These actions may deter my friends but I don't think it will stop criminals from breaking into my car or home. I float through life believing that all people are good, assuming the best of everyone.

Today, I attended a memorial service for a man who was not sure he believed in God. His daughter was Catholic, so the priest delivered a eulogy that gave her father entrance to the kingdom of heaven. I believe the church has to extinguish, or at least tone down, the fire and brimstone. The more theologically liberal population won't show up and listen to it. Donald, what do you think? Should I build a bomb shelter? Or just go to church more often?

On another note, what about that wall? Can all of the rich people in your administration help us to find the answers? If they are that rich, they must be pretty smart. I have a lot of faith in you to solve problems. I am either very naive or I am smarter than most people might think. Either way, Dale says I have angels watching out for me. I am hoping you are one of them.

HUMAN TRAFFICKING

July 23, 2017

Dear Donald,

My dad died on this day many years ago. So, I am thinking about him a lot today. The day of his funeral, the lead limousine guided the procession of cars past Dad's automobile dealership. This gave all of his employees working that day, the opportunity to pay tribute to him. The workers left the building, gathered at the curb and as the hearse passed, they placed their hands over their hearts.

My son, who was sitting next to me, was not much older than ten. Neither of us expected to drive by his place of work. I remember how deeply moved I was by it. Clearly, this man was loved and respected. Those who knew him expressed how generous and kind he was. I was so proud of him. I was grateful for the man he had been and the legacy he left behind. It was important for my son to see the tribute and hear all of the praises for his grandfather. My hope was that my son would remember this forever. And that it would inspire him to be a good man, one who cared about others and achieved much.

On this day, when I remember my dad, the stories on the news are overflowing with profound evil. ISIS is always a part of the narrative. Infighting between political parties is endless. Protests are angry and there is always a fear of violence erupting. The worst of it today was a story about human trafficking.

A huge truck from Mexico housed nearly one hundred men in their twenties and thirties and two school aged minors. They were packed into the back of the truck without water or air conditioning for a very long time. Because one of them managed to beg someone for water in a Walmart parking lot in San Antonio, Texas, a call was made to rescue these people.

The temperature in the back of the truck was over 150 degrees. Nine people were dead at the scene. Many were sick, vomiting and in danger of heat exhaustion resulting in brain damage. The driver will face state and federal charges and is likely connected to a larger ring of smugglers.

"Give me your tired, your poor..." I remember the words on the Statue of Liberty. My dad's plaque proudly faces the "Lady of American benevolence" who welcomed outsiders to the land at Ellis Island.

I thank God that Dad got into the United States safely and legally. I pray that while you protect all of us, you work with others to help these desperate souls. They are so longing to be welcomed by a "golden door" that will not swing open for them. Have mercy on those who risk being packed into deathly hot trucks and shipped like cheap cargo into our country.

I LOVE THE GUY

———

July 24, 2017

Dear Donald,

Anthony Scaramucci loves everybody with the possible exception of Jeff Sessions. You have been displeased lately with Sessions and the breaking news tonight is that he was talking too much about the campaign. Someone claims they overheard him talking with the Russians. Does it ever, ever end? *The Washington Post* is spinning the story and FOX NEWS is on top of it. I don't see much satire material in Scaramucci.

I am writing as I am watching the news. There are so many commercials, especially for drugs that will fix everything providing one doesn't experience side effects. Pills, potions and poisons are out there for anything that ails you. Whatever happened to the entertaining commercials like the dancing raisins?

Dale was watching TV in the man cave and came up to tell me about a breaking news story. Three teens took pictures of a man drowning and did nothing to help. They didn't even call for help! What is this world coming to? The Bible warned of the day when the very young would be cold and indifferent, so self absorbed that caring for others would not be possible.

The bottom line is we have approached the bottom line. Evil lurks everywhere and many are so overwhelmed that it can no longer be ignored. This callousness is prevalent in Washington. It is Democrats and Republicans, Northerners and Southerners, city dwellers and country folk. The children have lost their innocence and have become jaded and hard hearted.

Tomorrow, there is a religious rally at the Huntington Convention Center of Cleveland. It was organized by Christians who want the love of God to return to the culture, cities, country, children, government and the fallen. They are calling for all to return to the love of Christ. Calling all humans. Return to right living.

THE BOOKS

———————

July 25, 2017

Dear Donald,

I am doing my homework. I told you that the library listed over ninety books either by you or about you. I am going to check them all out. So far, I have been through seven. What a history! There is plenty of not so flattering research which some authors chose to emphasize. They can be brutal. It is, at times, painful for me to read the disparaging descriptions and interpretations of your life. I force myself to read all that is out there just to be informed.

There is no doubt that you have made plenty of mistakes and that you can act like a street fighter. There is no doubt that you are guilty of your share of narcissism. Who in this culture is not? Modern times have glorified fame and fortune. This "Hollywood" trend of the silver screen glamour has trickled down to the masses through social media.

High school yearbook photos have morphed into model cover shoots and cost fortunes. The young people being photographed, pose in dozens of fashion shots in elaborate settings. Soon, parents will fly their youngsters to Paris to seek more exciting locations to be photographed. Social media followers share every moment of their lives making the latest meal significant.

This "I am special" mania is addictive and this next generation will have to invent a new word to describe it. Instead of online social media, my generation protested for a minute when we were young and out of college. We hollered, "Make love, not war" and "Money isn't everything" at the top of our lungs. The flower children of the 60s have raised some very self-indulgent children.

Does it help that everyone gets awards and we do not tolerate champions? We are all stars and champions, our ribbons and trophies prove it. Children used to be given birthday parties on special years. Today, in many parts of the country, children are given a party every year. Some get several parties every year! Some of these parties are catered with entertainment at home or they are given at very expensive venues.

Most of us have bought into the culture of excess. We are to buy more, do more, go more, eat more, drink more, drug more. More, more, more! We push to prominence and significance. We went from meditating to mania. We are addicted to media and phones. I think we are the "swamp." Does God look down on us and lament, "Not one among you!" I know that God is kind and forgiving and for that I am grateful.

Redemption is in each of us. My pastor just named our new church The Redemption Center. We all need to find a better way. I wrote a song called, "Jesus Saves the Poor" and another called "Sister Salvation, She Stole Our Heart Away." We are both going to need God's grace to find and embrace a path that is honorable and worthy of God's blessing. Whatever time we have left in our lives, we must use it wisely.

GIANTS

Dear Donald,

On the news today I saw a clip of you from seventeen years ago! Even then, you were talking about negotiations with North Korea. You were sure that the dance there was real and needed to be addressed quickly and not let firm action wait. Nobody listened to you then. Now, every leader on the news looks exasperated and horrified at what North Korea is threatening. I think you are ahead of your time. I am an idealist and you are a realist. There is a place for the both of us in the running of this country. When one is faced with someone who is yelling like a Goliath with a giant weapon pointed at your land, reality is best. You need to kill the giant.

I would be sending the "Giant" flowers and gifts like Obama to Cuba. I would try to reason with him and pray. Like the people in Denmark, I would hug the terrorists and try to make them feel better. I would trust my unconditional love to melt the evil in their hearts, while embassy workers in San Juan lose their hearing and suffer strange symptoms of concussion.

I remember reading *Clockwork Orange*. I think I need to read it again. It is about the British who were duped by those who took advantage of government programs. My caring heart is needed in a healthy society. Thank God for your firm hand to make ours better. Without a balance of heart, strength, discipline, support and fairness, as a country, we are doomed.

Our children are spoiled and yet, we continue to do that. When that doesn't work, we spoil our grandchildren! Our culture doesn't care about the elderly nor do the elderly receive our respect. There is an assisted living facility in every town and neglected grandparents are on wait lists for care that is shabby, late and at times abusive. Family values have been traded for convenient community care, no matter what the financial, physical or emotional costs.

Convenience is the word of the day and it is paid care, day and night for the young and old. I am guilty of this pontificating about caring while I supported institutionalized "caring." We need to have strong family values again. The elderly should be revered for their wisdom and their importance in the family. Our children need a stronger family unit.

As Americans, we are allowing our children to be raised by strangers. Parents areforfeiting and children are being robbed of the sacred connection of attachment so important to emotional development. I understand that there are some who truly need these child care services. But I think the majority of those who use these conveniences are more concerned about making money while trying to raise children. Little do they want to understand that children need family more than huge homes, fancy cars and lots of stuff. I remember pictures of your kids who used to be on the floor of your office at Trump Tower and are now with you in the White House.

I took note of the reverence you felt for your father. I have noticed that you keep a framed picture of your mother and father behind you in the oval office.

PROTEST

August 12, 2017

Dear Donald,

The news today is all about protests in Virginia. David Duke, former KKK leader, attended a white nationalist protest in Charlottesville. He is making a nightmare out of the gathering that concerns the removal of the statue of Confederate Gen.Robert E. Lee. Charlottesville is the center of the conflict where people have been bussed in to protect the statue. A lot of ugly rhetoric is flying around and eight have been injured. Locals are packing their guns in sight. They carry legally as long as they don't conceal their weapons.

David Duke is a racist and shouts his belief as though the two of you are on the same page, believing the same things. Yikes! You do not support the thoughts or actions of David Duke or his kind. Confusion like this is toxic and needs to be denounced. You condemn Duke's point of view. Vice President Pence backs your message and Melania leads the pack with a soft plea for peace and love.

Misunderstanding is everywhere and Melania has the right idea. I called Kelli, my colleague, today as I have been avoiding a requested meeting with her and others concerning my publication. I wrote about my considerations, prayed about them and discussed them with my new publisher. After a good deal of reflection, I decided to call Kelli to apologize about unfinished business between us and discuss concerns about her proposed meeting. With a kind and gracious tone of voice, I requested that she call me so that I could clear up some issues before the meeting. I need time to reflect and prepare for my new publisher. I need to be comfortable about the meeting and that means that I am ready and prepared with an agenda.

Watching the hysteria in Virginiaon television and the utter insanity of uninformed and bigoted groups there and at the White House, confirms in my mind that careful preparation before confronting problems in a meeting is important. Fortunately, my meeting is with rational and spiritual people who wish for a calm and sane discussion as much as I do. I need to put a diplomatic hat on and tell the truth about my discomfort. Being open, honest and flexible allows me to meet my needs without being belligerent or uncooperative. This will be a productive gathering.

FIRE AND FURY

August 13, 2017

Dear Donald,

While you rant and rave about North Korea, and while riots escalate in Virginia, I can't help but notice that women on FOX NEWS seem to be using the same makeup artist. I am really jealous. I need to wallow in this for a while. The idea of nuclear war incited by your very bold retorts to North Korea, are too scary for me to embrace. Rather than be "whisked into a frenzy," I prefer to focus on the perfect eyebrows of all of the FOX female commentators.

They all have very long hair, or at the very least, very highly styled hair. Most of them are gorgeous, cross their legs incessantly and kick their very high heels in the direction of the cameras. I have thrown out my four and a half inch heels. This disturbs me. I walk around the house in my three inch heels in a stubborn tirade to hold onto my youth and beauty. I wobble a bit in my plethora of expensive shoes. With a lot of hard work and persistence, my right ankle will strengthen. I will not give up. I cannot do anything about North Korea but I can conquer my high heel crisis.

My cousin, Diane, has tactfully informed me that my current choice of lipstick is awful. She doesn't like the liner, it is too dark. I know this, Donald, but with all of my fretting about Argentina, Iran, Russia, China, North Korea, South Korea and now Guam, I haven't had the presence of mind to give my lipstick the attention it desperately needs.

The women on FOX NEWS have perfect lips! That makeup artist must cost a fortune, but even she (or he) is a little out of control. Sometimes, the eye makeup is pretty extreme and every one of these women is wearing false eyelashes. I have studied this very closely and discussed it with a lot of women. They are as inspired and annoyed as I am by these beautiful, overly made up, brilliant, ivy league talk show "news queens."

The news is loaded with high drama. The beauty of these "news queen" commentators has made watching the national and international drama more exciting than the soap opera, *As the World Turns!* WASHINGTON...STARRING DONALD TRUMP AND SUSAN LUCCI. The stories are so outrageous that they seem less believable than television high drama.

The riot victims are slowly dying in a Virginia hospital. Their loved ones are in agony. I cannot bear the pain of this endless turmoil around the world. All of the bags of makeup in my house can't cover up this pain. I look in the mirror and I see the pain in my face. I feel the pain in my heart. I push the pain away and bury it in sugar while I sit here in my almost high heels. It haunts me.

AUGUST MOON

August 14, 2017

Dear Donald,

   I am going to my writing workshop today. I am supposed to be inspired and encouraged to finish this book in just a few weeks. It is not working. The more the workshop leader urges the group to write at least three pages a day, the less I write. I don't have writer's block, I have a bit of what might be called "writer's heartbreak."

   The news is so dispiriting that I can barely bring myself to write about it. South Korea is launching what looks like an atomic war, Argentina is falling apart and sending drugs to the US through Cuba. The Russians are furious with us, throwing out our diplomats, Obamacare is falling apart with no replacement in sight, Comey just got a two-million-dollar book deal and you hired retired Marine Corps General John Kelly as White House Chief of Staff to get some order at the White House.

   I learned that the General's son, who was a Marine, died in Afghanistan. How does this man find the spirit to go on fighting for us? My son is alive and well but there is great geographical distance between us. I do not see him as often as I would like, but at least I do see him. I know he is well. We FaceTime and he smiles and laughs. He records my grandchildren's swim meets, drumming, Lacrosse games and pizza fests. My grandsons show me their latest acquisitions and perform their new antics. I am sure that General Kelly is proud of his son for his service and sacrifice for our country. He does not have what I have. I should always be grateful for what I have because one never knows the future.

I want my kids underfoot all day long. Like you, I want to live with them and work with them being a huge positive influence in their lives. Sometimes it just isn't possible. My sister's kids circle her house waiting for what will come out of the oven or for what she has prepared and frozen for them. They worship her for the food! My mother and mother-in-law had the talent to cook wonderful memory making food! My daughter-in-law is a great cook, too! It's not that I don't have the ability, I'm just not into it. These women are brilliant at keeping family close at hand.

I am feeling fragile today. I forget how strong you are and how much you have accomplished. Like Humpty Dumpty, I fear that it will all fall apart. I have forgotten all of my accomplishments and in a vulnerable and lonely mood, I am allowing the fear of loss to overtake me. You have not fallen off of the wall. Congress will find a way to get the states to figure out the healthcare issue. The taxes will be handled, China will work with us, South Korea will calm down, your kids will be brilliant by your side and Democrats will be less hostile. These are everyone's problems but mostly, because you are President, they are yours. So, you manage these issues and I will do what I have the ability to control.

I will make plans to spend time with my son's family in

September and I will fit into my blue dress by then. I will stay healthy. We will all see one another again to laugh and be proud and celebrate great successes. I have to believe this or I will not be able to cope. I know I am supposed to live in the present and not fear the future or worse, long for it. Anyone who has ever missed their children knows how reasonable my unreasonable attitude is. And then there is General Kelly. There are no platitudes or words of comfort to offer him. I should be glad that I miss my family until I see them in September. I guess that is more than a lot of people have.

KOREAN NIGHTMARE

———

August 15, 2017

Dear Donald,

Why am I relieved to see you holding your arms and holding your ground against North Korea? You warned them to "stand down" or they will see a reaction of such hostile power, the likes of which the world has never seen. I am so sick of hearing about Russia and special councils snooping around for a rat, for anything that will weaken you or cast a doubt on your administration. I am still upset today and I have been for a number of days. Do you ever get upset? I know you have been furious, obsessed and concerned, but have you ever been teary?

I guess I have some regrets, some "what ifs." It is confusing being a woman in today's world. There is no way to win. No matter how successful, devoted to your home, how beautiful, strong, talented or ordinary, there is always someone who thinks you are doing it wrong. I am devoted to my work. Maybe I am still trying to prove to my dad that all of the money spent on my education wasn't wasted.

———

My dad adored all of his children. But, I know my dad favored my sister, Shirley. Why wouldn't he? She has infectious laughter and had a genuine concern for him. I, on the other hand, stood against the stereotype of women in the Lebanese culture. I wonder to this day if that rebellion made any sense. In this culture, when married, "You made your own bed." You know the rest of that saying! No matter now broken a marriage was, a good woman never divorced.

Do you question your divorces? I still drag around this notion that if only I had done this or that or did the other, the broken would mend. You don't seem to do that. You renegotiate and move on. Do you regret your past relationships? It seems that with you, what is done is done. There is work to do. Am I getting too personal?

I feel like a broken record but I can't imagine what it is like for you, Donald Trump, to be the President. Every day, no matter what you do, hundreds of millions of people find fault with you. So, you surround yourself with your supporters. Brilliant! I am going to surround myself with only people who hold me with high esteem. Dale, my significant other does most of the time. My friend Stuart adores me but he has been too busy to answer my calls. My cousins are supportive but they feel upset too. I grab my pillow and hope that a good nap will clear my head. All the while I trust that you, my Braveheart, will make America great again.

A TEN

August 16, 2017

Dear Donald,

Last Sunday at church, the sermon focus was on the number ten. So many times in the Bible, the number ten denotes power. There are the Ten Commandments. Why not six or eight? If a woman is considered a "knockout" she is described as being a "10." What is it about that number that seems to communicate the ultimate? My Pastor pointed out that the passage of scripture, "I can do all things through Christ who strengthens me" is a sentence with ten words. He hoped that pointing that out would help us to remember the passage throughout the week. It came to mind today as my heart has been heavy for a few weeks. I guess I did remember it.

I stepped on the toes of some colleagues this week. It was a bit of a mess. Like you, I had to ask myself if I abandoned them or they abandoned me? I read between the lines of your life for support. I heard you denounce the KKK and none of the statements that you made on camera or on Twitter made me doubt your words.

You never admit that you are wrong. But when people are angry, at you or about something else, they react in extreme ways. You are the scapegoat and vitriol is spewed at you for everything you say and don't say. People believe unkind things about you, that may be true or imagined, to fuel their anger.

There was nothing wrong about pointing out that both sides of the protests in Charlotte posed threats to the safety and well-being of those who attended. Violence is not acceptable by any party at a protest. There were a lot of violent personalities and other people who were genuinely concerned. Everyone wants you to denounce the KKK. And you did. For some, it wasn't good enough. What a surprise.

On the news I learned that for now, North Korea is backing down. Stand up to China, Russia, Iran, Mexico and Venezuela. I think they will want to know what you have to say to them. What if we all stopped making one another wrong? Wars are fought defending what is believed to be right on each side! What if we let go of black and white and held on to red, white and blue? Here are ten words for you:

ONE NATION UNDER GOD WITH LIBERTY AND JUSTICE FOR ALL!

Getting along can be hard work. It takes time, repeated dialogue, patience, listening and a willingness to understand another perspective. It takes a decision to forgive and put the past to rest, not forgetting it, but not giving it power. How do we emancipate ourselves from the shackles of our past sins and wounds? Ten words, "I can do all things through Christ who strengthens me." Good and meaningful words for all sides to digest to make peace within anxious hearts, that will change our world.

HELL ON WHEELS

August 17, 2017

Dear Donald,

Well, another rented van driven by terrorists has barreled through the crowded streets of Barcelona, that beautiful city in Spain. Hospitals are under siege as they try to attend the victims. Many are dead. I can't imagine that the solution is getting rid of motor vehicles. What is the answer to all of this? If you knew, I know you would fix it.

Today, my grandson's dog died peacefully at a quiet home in Ohio. My grandson heard about it in New York and was not able to hug his beloved dog and cry with his sweet tears to say good bye. The dog couldn't move to New York with his family. There was no room in crowded apartments or rented homes in New York. It is so hard to lose a pet. Sometimes pets make the best of friends.

Lucas is now twelve. He is courageous and a champion of many things, especially swimming. But he is afraid to fly. When I went to New York to see him in a talent show, he was overwhelmed that

I would risk my life to see him. I am sad that Lucas fears flying but I am not surprised. Lucas sees the scenes as they unfold around the world. His television is on or the news is flashed on his iPhone. The world in turmoil is pulling families apart. If families stayed closer, I think we would feel safer.

The need for our children to move from their home towns to other cities to find work may be nothing new but it feels new to me and to others who were brought up in families where togetherness mattered. I remember meeting a woman who was grieving that her child and grandchildren moved to another city. She felt lonely and empty and was eating her way through her pain.

Years later, I had the same experience. I mourned. I forget that my family may have mourned the separation from me, the loss of their beautiful home, friends and their precious pet. It was a grief for all. As Carole King put it, "I felt the earth move under my feet." Now I understand her words in a visceral way.

My cousins are hosting their yard sale today and selling precious memories for pennies. They are too old to drag the past around with them. It is so sad to see sentimental treasures being driven away by strangers.

We are all moving from place to place and decade to decade, we hold on to one another with as much tenacity as we can muster. This is a culture where Facebook and Twitter and television coverage of world news keeps us reeling. We can hardly feel our feelings.

A van mows over a crowd of innocents and we stop just for a moment to mourn. My feelings turn inward and I chant, "I will not be afraid" while my children move so fast to stay afloat in an ever changing dangerous world. Are they too dizzy to admit that they are disappointed in the way the world is playing out in the twenty-first century? Or, is it their world and they understand the risks of adventure and are willing to take them? Maybe to them, this world is a good place that is filled with mostly kind and honest people with a few bad apples in the basket. Perhaps it has always been that way and it is just my perception that is haunting.

From my vantage point, now that we can all virtually travel at unthinkable speed, I am beginning to wonder why anyone would risk going anywhere at all.

NO PEACE

_____

August 19, 2017

Dear Donald,

Thirty-five thousand people marched in Boston for all kinds of opposing ideas. The Boston police had a very effective response to the crowds. For the most part, the masses were peaceful. There were some pretty rough reactions to those wearing your famous red caps. Anger was real, but contained. There was hope in my heart as I watched the marches over the hours. America could agree to disagree and keep negotiating. Then, shots were fired killing police officers in other places in our country. I am beginning to wonder if the entire country is a bit insane. What is the definition of insanity?

Negotiation can be a long and painful process and few do it effectively and efficiently. It is not easy to stand up for your rights when someone across the table is yelling. We are a culture in need of coaching in conflict resolution.

I had another run-in with colleagues this week. I was wrong and so were they. The obvious problems were not the real problems, those have been unspoken for years. Several publishers needed conversations because their work often overlapped, they were so busy, overworked and under deadline pressures. Interactions were avoided or postponed. Each had a way of looking at their work which was different from the others and there wasn't time enough to sort it out. Even though I have a certificate in conflict resolution, I am often too overwhelmed or intimidated to employ the concepts.

Thought and time can help. When I was a teacher, I asked the Principal for some advice regarding a conflict at work. His response was, "Give the situation some time. Time takes time." He suggested that I give the situation some thought, journaling, prayer and meditation. I will never forget that.

What bothers me is that conflict never stops occurring. If you are alive and interacting, there will be differences of opinion, style, philosophies and values. The smartest people alive have conflicts. Conflict has been around since the dawn of time. When viewed in proper perspective, it makes life interesting. What would life be like if everyone thought and acted like me?

Dale just repeated all of the necessary steps that need to be taken to slice a tomato. He told me the way I do it leaves the counter a mess and needs to be cleaned up. I wanted to get out of his way because he doesn't like to trip over me while he works in the kitchen. I got out of his way and I left the counter a bit messy. After he counseled me in proper kitchen behavior, he broke a glass. Need I say more?

ECLIPSE

August 20, 2017

Dear Donald,

Thank heavens for the eclipse. All the stations were talking about it and focusing on that special moment when the moon passed between the earth and the sun. I needed a break from the anti-Trumpism that is relentless from the Democrats. Byron York reported today on TV that the Republicans are raising twice as much money as the Democrats. This generosity comes from small donors despite all of the negative press.

Even though your supporters don't always agree with you, they trust your heart because they trust their own. They want liberty and justice for all and to end prejudice and crime. They hope all Americans will have a voice, a good job or career, a happy life and a constructive way to contribute to society. We all want lower taxes and a break for the middle class. Veterans need to be treated like the heroes they are. Military strength is important. North Korea needs to settle down and there should be security against ISIS and illegal immigration. Legal immigrants should be welcomed and properly vetted. Your supporters want a healthcare system that really works, makes sense and is affordable. They want fair trade, an end to failing cities and schools and a lower national debt. They want to drain the swamp.

Jerry Lewis died today. He held a grudge against Dean Martin for twenty years. Jerry raised over two billion dollars for charity. We are all pretty complicated. There is a saint and sinner in all fo us. People on both sides of the aisle pray for you because most Americans, I believe, are more saintly and lean to their higher selves. Many who do not agree with you are not marching, yelling, insulting or undermining you. Multitudes are waiting and watching, hoping you can succeed and bring the country together.

Tomorrow you will give a national address relating to policies concerning Afghanistan. What miraculous words can you utter to soften the hate that is out there? What will you say to inspire sanity in a divided country? One speech cannot solve the problems that have accumulated through the decades. Your speech will be different. You will speak light and truth to your people. It will be a ray of sunshine to what seems like an endless eclipse of the heart. Speak hope to anyone who will listen. With God's help, let the sun shine in.

MY NAME "ECLIPSE"

August 21, 2017

Dear Donald,

After watching the eclipse yesterday, I was told by my cousin Judy Kassouf, that my father's last name, "Kassouf" means "eclipse." I grew up thinking that the name meant "stone cutter." Judy differs. She told all of my cousins to look it up and sure enough, it means "eclipse." For the first time, I fully related to the young black woman on television who had her DNA tested. She bashfully admitted that she spit into a sample kit and sent it in to discover her heritage. She then located a ceremonial hat that dripped African charm and represented her ancestry. She tearfully and joyfully perched it upon her head. "It's a hat," she exclaimed, as if to apologize for getting so excited about this adornment. Her sentiment was visceral.

My black girlfriend, Gale, tells me that many black people are still lugging around the names of their slave owners. Once in slavery, they lost touch with their roots and did not know their real names. I bought some makeup a few weeks ago from a beautiful black woman who worked at Sephora, a makeup store at the mall. Her name was "Aqua." Suddenly, hearing this name, I understood the need for such unusual names among my black friends such as Lamar, Yoshi and Tari. To have an ancestral name is sacred; to name yourself is divine.

I was buying makeup to perfectly finish a gorgeous royal blue outfit I was putting together for a wedding. My dear friend wanted me to "dress to kill" for her big day. She has approved of every accessory to my outfit and is delighting in my "pulling out the stops."

The "Kentucky Derby" hat designer piled cascades of royal blue roses to drip from a sheer picture hat. The royal blue sheath dress has inspired weeks of dieting and exercise. The royal blue satin opera gloves may be too much. We'll see. And yes, Cinderella Eclipse has, if not glass slippers, royal blue velvet high heels. While beautiful "Aqua" carefully applied long lashes to my eyelids, I wondered if I might change my name to "Royal Blue"? For a moment, the idea was thrilling.

"What's in a name? A rose is still a rose." Names describe us. So many things that we do and say let the world know who we are. My family name has the power to let me know who I am. Cousin Judy has graced me with the notion that I am powerful, mystical and rare, like an eclipse.

In Genesis, of the common testament of the Bible, God changed the name of Sarai to Sarah, meaning a princess, the mother of all nations. Similarly, her husband Abram was renamed to Abraham meaning the father of a multitude. To change a name often changes an identity and maybe even destiny! I am not limited by the name given to me by my family. Only God knows who I am and who I can be! I can do all things with God's help.

Years ago, my dear cousin Karin Kassouf reminded me that I was more than my name, my past and my mistakes. She reminded me with her precious Christian spirit, that as a child of God, I am the "daughter of a king." Well, then, perhaps you might just call me "Princess Royal Blue."

WRITTEN IN STONE

August 23, 2017

Dear Donald,

You were not "presidential" in Phoenix. It was 115 degrees and over ten thousand people waited for you in the sweltering heat. You signed autographs for an hour in the hot sun. You breezed up and down the steps of Air Force One with ease. You don't let the negative press or the unruly protestors get in your way. You are with your friends, your fans and you let your hair down. You let it "all hang out" and your fans love it. Many in the television audience love it too. But we wait and wince, thinking there is an "oh, no" moment coming or a "yikes, he went too far" moment. We know that tomorrow your opposition audience is going to tear this apart all day long, despite your popularity.

Will the "real crazy" please stand up? Robert Lee, a gentleman of Asian descent, could not announce a game in Charlotte because his name might offend a hostile audience. They might mistake poor Robert for a Confederate statue. The man is Asian! This is way too much. I'm all for revisiting the issues of the statues. I just want us to slow down a bit and talk and talk and talk about the issues. Then, decide after a fair and lengthy discourse.

In my mind, success comes from hard work and endless persistence. The artists who were chosen to make the statues worked hard on them. That needs to be considered too. I am willing to consider that these statues can be one of a million pieces to the puzzle that builds a picture of oppression. I respect those who fight for these issues while they are working hard at their jobs, studies and loving relationships. There is room to be a "change agent" in America without raising your fist or throwing a brick through a window.

In Phoenix, you were ranting and raving and letting all of your honest feeling be heard. In speeches to the military, you were measured, noble and elegant. Both of these speeches were truly you. You are who you are. I know that I can trust one thing. What I hear from you is authentically, you. Your public has not yet become accustomed to your very wide range. You hit high notes, low notes, eager and eloquent notes. One minute, you can shout it out in street talk. The next, you pour your most passionate and lofty thoughts out in elevated discourse.

Statues embrace a man in a moment. We'll have to memorialize you in some other way. You move too fast and are too complex for us to capture your essence in clay.

MISSOURI

August 30, 2017

Dear Donald,

Welcome to Missouri! Days of painful flooding in Texas and Louisiana left millions wet, sick, dead, shivering and overwhelmed. You flew into the flooded area and dressed down. So many criticized you and your lovely wife for wearing black and white casual attire with caps and sneakers. You looked like two rich kids ready to go off to school. I know you meant well. How do kings and queens appear at places that experienced disaster? In Missouri you caught your breath. However, it is difficult to concentrate on tax programs while so many are in turmoil in Houston and beyond.

So far, you have been very strong and organized about the storms and floods. You were kind, concerned, compassionate and appropriate. Your sincerity is real and most of us understand it. You extended every grace to the storm victims and places in need before you moved on to previous commitments in Missouri. We must address the crises in the aftermath of the floods as we continue to address the future of our country.

The Mayor of Port Arthur, TX, waded through many feet of water in his home. A shelter is flooded with gushes of water with frogs floating above the submerged cots. If this isn't enough to bear, the reporter announced that a great-grandfather, his wife and four great grandchildren drowned in the storm. A nurse on the TV screen sobbed at a nursing home where she mourned the suffering of the frightened elderly residents as they are waist deep in dirty, cold water. People have snakes in their homes.

In the rest of the world, the societal and cultural storms remain relentless. North Korea rages on. Venezuela is falling apart. ISIS takes a moment off and more than likely celebrates all of the damage done to the US without their help. Evil abounds in nature, nations, cults and criminals.

Thank you, Missouri, for a moment of peace and sanity. This madness will go on for weeks and yet, we are already weary from the devastation. Maybe the storm is a metaphor for the mood of our country. We are flooded with rage from disappointments. We are exhausted from searching for common ground. We are defensive as we hold fast to our stands. We are stubborn and fed up with the complications of trying to get along. We are drowning in defiance, self-pity and impatience.

What is the message from Mother Nature? Maybe it is that we need to reach out to each other with sincere mutual concern. We must not drown in our hate but save each other with our love.

RECOVERY

September 2, 2017

Dear Donald,

The public has not been kind to Melania. She doesn't know what to do with a cap and sneakers. The left is vicious, finding fault with her every outfit, word, action and non-action. They criticize her husband, son, accent and wardrobe. She will survive, and so will Texas.

Hurricane Harvey was the worst storm the US has ever experienced. The damage is devastating. Texas Congressman Randy Weber says that in a strange way, the hurricane has brought out the better natures of our people. Texas will recover, the people are resilient.

These days, you are showing a softer side and Melania is trying to be "one of us." Ted Cruz is working respectfully and appreciatively with you. Soon, we will learn the plan for the "Dreamers." After watching your compassion this week, many are persuaded you are going to do your best to treat them with the "heart" you promised.

Some fear that our differences in the country right now will tear us apart. Some predict another civil war. Some struggle with murderous anger. Others suffer from unbearable disappointment. We have differences that we can negotiate. We cannot negotiate with a storm or while staring down the barrel of a gun. There is hope and there is potential for getting along. Potential is the silver lining. Hopefully we will see the light of common good.

Today, apart from the tragedies of the world, my friend Gale and I enjoyed a safe and friendly morning. We went to a meeting together. She is black and a Democrat. I am white and at least for now, a Republican. We talk politics and differences in our cultures and races. We do it peaceably in a context of respect and concern for each other. Her daughter is a lesbian. I have a friend who is gay and Jewish. Gale and I are strong Christians. We love talking about different points of view and we learn so much. For us, the cultural, race, orientation storm is over. We have weathered our differences and celebrated our common desire to get along. Thank goodness.

PARADISE

September 3, 2017

Dear Donald,

Tomorrow is Labor Day. If it is warm, I will go to the neighborhood pool and get a little sun. I will get back to the hot water pool Tuesday to do my water exercises. We have a great recreation center in my town, as do most towns in northeast Ohio. When I moved from New York back to Cleveland, I was amazed by the many elaborate recreation centers available to town residents. I belong to mine for $88 a year. I wonder why Long Island didn't have this luxury? The local taxes here cover the costs and residents are delighted with the amenities. We have pools, exercise classes, gyms with steam rooms, games and programs for seniors, tracks, outdoor play areas and sun decks. There is abundant outdoor space for teams and events.

Suddenly, my town in Ohio that is free of hurricane damage feels like paradise! We are not flooded or forced out of our homes. The water is clean and the stores are filled to capacity with food and clothing. Our appliances are working and cars are

---

undamaged. Water is clean and plentiful. Gas prices are up a bit but nobody is complaining as we watch and wait on recovery in Texas.

I had out of town guests last week and we toured the great city of Cleveland. We went to the Rock and Roll Hall of Fame and to lovely restaurants overlooking the bridges that span the Cuyahoga River. We rode on an open-air tour bus for two and a half hours. My guests marveled at how clean the city was. The sky was blue, the breeze was perfect, the city abounded with flowers and fountains at every turn.

My guest, Barbara, saw my home and assessed that it would cost three to four times the price in New York. While scouting my house, she noticed hat boxes stacked in my bedroom closet and asked to try the hats on. Soon, there were boxes all over the house and we were taking pictures of her in every millinery creation. I sent her home with her favorite. I haven't cleaned up the mess yet. I live in awe and gratitude for the endless abundance of having a home, shelter, safety, water, food and hats, of all things, in every color.

I pray for our country and for the beautiful state of Ohio. I take my cowboy hat off to Texas. I pray for the people there and donated towards the recovery. I have been watching them face this storm with courage, strength, sanity and grace. God bless Texas tough.

TAXES AND STORMS

———————

September 6, 2017

Dear Donald,

"It's not going to happen. Let me tell you." This is one of your favorite lines and you used it over and over in North Dakota as you spoke to the citizens about the drought they recently endured. You are with Ivanka and I am so excited for her. She is embracing the work and missions of the White House, watching and learning. She is impeccable in her presentation. She always seems to wear the perfect outfit and express herself with warmth and good taste. I ordered a pair of her heels on Amazon and they are gorgeous. I was surprised at how moderately priced they were. She is reaching out to real people in her marketing and I think that is very smart.

You talk about tax cuts while the television screen highlights in the lower right corner a box that tracks hurricane Irma. Irma and Harvey have been nightmares. I feel frozen. It is difficult to get business moving as everyone is holding their collective breath to see which way the storm will move. Will it be a category 3, 4 or 5?

Recovery from these disastrous storms will take a long time. My calm friend Stuart even feels like the world is coming to an end.

It seems there are storms everywhere. North Korea is a raging storm of ominous threats. Irma is still blowing at 185 mph. DACA is in crisis while the Senate figures out, or not, what to do with the "Dreamers" and those related to them.

With all of this, Ivanka's blonde hair is blowing in the Dakota wind. You are in a constant state of confidence that it will all be great. We are going to make America great again no matter how fierce the winds or how high the water.

I feel like I am on hold. Waiting. In reality, the storm is strengthening. I do feel there has been a shift between the Democrats and Republicans. I feel that both sides of the aisle are more willing to listen and make some compromises. You worked with Chuck Schumer and Nancy Pelosi and the storm was suddenly a breath of fresh air. Smart move, Donald. You know how to make a deal. And you did.

THE SPIN

September 7, 2017

Dear Donald,

Your agreement with Chuck Schumer and Nancy Pelosi about the debt ceiling is causing the usual stir. Some are praising it, others are using it to make themselves look good, like Mr. Schumer who implies that he is an amazing deal maker. They apparently don't know about The Art of the Deal, by none other than you! Or, maybe that is where he learned to deal! The Republicans are not happy. The Democrats are trying to make it look like you caved. I have no idea about anyone's thinking or strategy.

I had a meeting today with the radio station that wants to air my show. The marketing options were so confusing to me that I felt like I had been thrown into quicksand. I could sell my own advertising, or not. I could retain ownership of the show, or not. I could get someone to partner with me who was gifted in marketing shows like mine and taping products that a partner could sell into other radio markets. I could do the show with a co-person or not. The producer said these options were up to me.

With all of this information swirling in my head, all I wanted was a bowl of Cheerios. When I feel overwhelmed, I want to stuff my feelings while I try to sort things out. I decided to be simply honest. I am really good at what I do, but the entire marketing end of the show is not at all appealing to me. Some people have great talent for marketing. I can create the show. Marketing overwhelms me. The station executive was quick to assess who I was and who I was not. I was given all kinds of ideas that he thought would support the growth of my show. After a clear discussion he said, "Give me a few days and I'll get back to you." My sense of all this is, he believed in me and he intended to find a way for it to succeed.

Sometimes, I just need to rely on God to work out the deal. There are doors I do not know how to open. There are constructive steps to take, but I do not know what they are. I didn't have the time or inclination to market the show or to sell time. I trusted and believed in my own very real talent to create endless content on uplifting topics. I have that charm and inspiration in abundance. I am like a gushing oil well of treasures. But, once the oil gushes, someone else will have to take it to the market. The complexities of today's electronic and social media will have to be managed by someone else. No spin here, just an honest sit down.

ROBBED

September 8, 2017

Dear Donald,

The storm hasn't hit yet, but already I am feeling robbed. I have held on to a Florida condo which belonged to my parents. The condo is on the Gulf coast, on Boca Ciega Bay in St. Petersburg. Miami Dade has forty shelters open. A few days ago, I thought the storm was headed to the East Coast, but now it has turned westward.

In the forty years that my St. Pete Beach condo has been in the family, it suffered damage from only one storm. The kitchen floor and carpeting had to be replaced in the 6th floor apartment. We used huge fans to dry out the little bit of water that blew in from the sliding doors. At that time, I was living on Long Island and had good insurance for the Florida property. The insurance company cancelled my insurance the following year. It took me a while to replace it.

The debt ceiling is going to be higher now that all of this relief money will be going to the states hit by these hurricanes. This

---

is devastation for so many. Even the wealthy are facing risk. The storm doesn't play favorites. Hurricanes can wipe out trailers or mansions, campgrounds or first-class hotels. Your Mar-a-Lago could be demolished.

I feel robbed of time, safety and resources each time one of these terrible hurricanes hits the country. I cannot concentrate on moving forward with my "to do" list. Right now, I am fixed on following the path of Irma.

I have always lived near water and there is a price to pay when the hurricanes howl. I loved living in New York in Port Washington, a sailing town. When 9-11 hit New York, it was like a hurricane. New York was never the same for me. I was always looking over my shoulder for a terrorist.

Now I live on a small pond in Ohio. I feel very safe here, but sad. I miss my friends and family and all of the excitement of NYC. I have friends and family here too, but the longer I live, I realize that life is about celebrating the day while you fasten your seatbelt and look both ways. There is no safe place. Safety really is a myth.

I remember hearing a story about a man who moved his family to a quiet town to get away from the risks and hassles of the big city. His innocent child was one who was killed in Columbine.

Each day we awaken with the possibility of being robbed of our finances, reputation, possessions and health by intruders, natural disasters or by sickness and disease. We can also awaken to the possibility of being celebrated. A nurse in Florida won the lottery for almost a billion dollars. On the same day, a man is killed trying to install hurricane shutters. Most of us live in the middle of these extremes negotiating the good days and those that aren't so good. Celebrate the days you can. Choose faith, fun and friendship. I called my friends in the path of the storm and prayed for them.

Over all, even today, "This is the day that the Lord has made. Rejoice and be glad in it."

THE WEDDING

September 15, 2017

Dear Donald,

Tomorrow, I attend the wedding of a dear young friend, Kelly. She is my hairdresser and has been in my magazine for many years. I have played a really important role in building her business. She owns a salon in Hudson, Ohio where she does very high-end glamorous hairstyling.

Kelly has been sending me pictures on Facebook and from her phone as she gets ready for her big day! She looks so happy as she has been counting down the days to her "here comes the bride" moment. The service will be held outside facing Lake Erie in Vermillion. The venue looks like a high-end log cabin. There are 180 steps from the venue to the outside altar. I know this because I chatted with the staff. I needed to know because I am planning to wear heels, shoes I haven't worn in a very long time. I don't want to dress down for this event.

I have been hobbling around the house for months training myself to wear heels again after two hip replacements. I got my

---

weight under control and bought a half dozen dresses before finally putting together an outfit I feel beautiful wearing. The hat requires courage. It cascades with bold blue roses and tulle. It will be a sunny and breezy day but chilly. The person at the venue warned me to bring a sweater. I will have a blue and black fox muff. I will wear heels that are nearly four inches high. They will look wonderful with my sheathe dress. As long as I stay with Dale and know his arm to lean on is close, I am confident that I can manage. I am nervous about it, but happy and proud that I fought my way back to what is normal for me.

When I walk joyfully down the aisle to my seat, I will pray that I can be fully present for the ceremony. As the wedding begins, hurricane Irma will have pounded its way to the Gulf Coast where my empty condo awaits the impact. I pray that it passes through without destroying my place or hurting my cousins huddled behind boarded up homes in Ft. Meyers. Behind where they live is a pond that is full of alligators. What do they do in a category five hurricane?

I know you have that lovely estate, Chateau des Palmiers, in St. Martin. And then there is Mar-a-Lago. I pray for your properties and I ask that you pray for mine. Let's hope that the damage is minimal and that lives are spared.

SISTER

Dear Donald,

I know how much you love and respect your sister, the former federal judge. You often speak with great affection for your brother who died from a struggle with alcoholism. I think you just welcomed your 9th grandchild into the family. What a blessing! One of the things that I admire most about you is your devotion to your family. All of your children and grandchildren seem to love, respect and admire you.

One of my sisters died several years ago. She was the eldest. Her name was Vonni and she promised me that she was going to Heaven. I asked, "How will I know you are in Heaven? Send me a picture." Vonni was an artist and I had such fond memories of the pictures she created while I was growing up. She won contests for her outstanding work. She told me she would send me a picture of Heaven. How would that happen? Whimsical requests deserve whimsical answers!

After her death, in a matter of weeks, all three of her children visited me. Without the knowledge of the others, each one arrived with a different picture they wanted me to have. Tammy came with a painting Vonni had in her bedroom for many years. It belonged to my parents and I loved it. It was a painting of a very young woman holding a very young child. I hung it in the dining room and Dale stared at it for a while. He wondered if it was a picture of Vonni holding me. I looked more carefully and the older girl did look like Vonni when she was young.

Vonni's son arrived with his picture for me. It was a photograph that he had taken in Florida from the balcony of my condo overlooking Boca Ciega Bay. It was beautiful and it also went in the dining room.

Finally, the third child, Amy, arrived with a photograph of Vonni holding my son, Dennis, shortly after he was born. This touching photograph also went in the dining room.

Well, Vonni, in her special way surely did deliver pictures from Heaven. These were my miracle messages I had asked for. Miracles abound, Heaven is real. Picture that.

SHEA

September 23, 2017

Dear Donald,

My family and a lot of my friends voted for you. I winced a little when you used the tag "Rocket Man" to describe the leader of North Korea. Dale loved it. The women in the family worry about you and all of the opposition that you are facing. The men are fed up with the negativity too.

This week I am planning a birthday party for my sister Shirley. We affectionately call her Shea. The grandchildren coined that nickname when they couldn't pronounce her name. Shea's name is Shirley Ann on her birth certificate. The Lebanese word for grandmother is "Sito." The toddlers scrambled all of this and came up with Shea.

Shea is a great cook. I avoid cooking as I am always watching my weight. The less time I spend focusing on food, the better. Anytime I visit Shea, I am inspired by her creativity with cooking. Her new kitchen is beautiful and pristine. White on white requires meticulous care and relentless organization. Shea is always on top of it.

Her family delights in her culinary skills. She knows everyone's favorites and makes them all, at one time or another. Needless to say, when that oven door closes, family flocks to the kitchen. They know that in just a matter of time that their taste buds will be tantalized. Shea always makes more than enough so her guests can take home packages filled with leftovers of the delightful repast. There is no sibling rivalry here. There is no competing with this talent. The blue ribbon belongs to her!

Shea has experienced her share of pain and suffering. She has buried loved ones, friends and family. She worries about the welfare of her children in this politically unstable climate and that of the world. She has concerns for her grandchildren. Her marriage has had its share of challenges. In spite of all of this, she laughs. There is something magical about her that is different from anyone else in the family. Her laughter is more beautiful and captivating than any talent one could imagine. Nothing robs her of this gift from God. She can embrace life fully with all of the joys, sorrows, trials and tribulations that are part of the package. And yet, she laughs, quietly, hysterically and often. Of all of the dishes she conjures up, nothing is more delicious than her laughter. "Joy hath a continual feast." Happy Birthday Shea and keep laughing.

THE WALL

_____

September 24, 2017

Dear Donald,

Robert Frost did not like walls. Have you read his poem "Mending Wall?" The Berlin Wall was a nightmare. The Great Wall of China has always felt pretty scary to me. Aren't we supposed to build bridges and not walls? It is no wonder there are so many mixed feelings about this very expensive and somewhat intimidating wall. Dr. Emerson Eggerichs became famous because of his best seller, Love and Respect. It taught me how to have a working, successful relationship with a man. He has released a new book which warns us to watch out before we push the send button. Be sure that what you are sending is true and kind. The idea of a wall is kind to us in some ways and mean in others. We are welcoming to legals and threatening to intruders and criminals. The great Statue of Liberty boasts, "Give me your tired, your poor, your huddled masses yearning to breathe free." America can't handle all who want to enter. And some are cruel and dangerous.

There needs to be middle ground. The love and respect thing has morphed into hypocritical political correctness. We are told to tolerate that which often should not be tolerated. And sometimes, political correctness is a double-edged sword. We are told not to body shame people who are "weighty." But this has enabled our country to excuse dangerous obesity.

Our descriptions and conversations are sugar coated. We wonder why the millennials are soft and need coloring books, safe rooms on campuses and therapy dogs for comfort. Most of us are nauseated by this epidemic of political correctness. It puts us at risk. There is a generation or two out there who cannot cope with normal life events, pleasant or unpleasant. We need to toughen our skins a bit. Life isn't always fair and sometimes it really hurts. One thing I've learned, it goes on.

I am guilty of being kind to a fault. I passed being plain sugar sweet and moved on to glucose. You are less than kind when you are blunt. We all need to stop spreading sweet frosting over life's sour realities.

Today, I respect the need for stronger borders, walls, boundaries and limits. Can we be honest without being brutal? Can we face truth without running to a safe zone to the coloring books, hot cocoa and therapy puppies? Can hearts be opened and still build supportive walls of protection? Some walls are sacred. The Wailing Wall in Jerusalem holds the prayers of millions. Our wall in America needs to be built carefully, one prayerful brick at a time.

HOPE

Dear Donald,

September is almost over and we have had a rough one. Hurricanes, storms, earthquakes, fires and threats of more have dominated the news for many weeks. There is a sadness everywhere these devastating events have happened. My condo in Florida was badly hit and while the repairs are well underway, there will be some nice upgrades to the apartment. My grieving for the thousands who have endured terrible losses is juxtaposed with many happy events.

Earlier this month, my friend Kelly got married. I dressed to kill for her wedding and that was fun for me. Although I felt the pressure of being perfect for her for her day, with the news looming, my zest was unseemly. I felt a bit guilty fussing over hats, shoes and other adornments while so many suffered the effects of mother nature.

I hosted a luncheon at my home for some women from my sorority. I gave a presentation about women to the retired female teachers who were present. My house was filled with flowers and a charming pianist played my baby grand throughout lunch. My talk was better than I thought it would be. Joy! At my sister's birthday party, I presented her a page from my Dear Donald book. She was thrilled because it was about her! She said she would frame it. How fabulous is that? Growing up we shared a room with twin beds.

The world was watching when you and the leader of North Korea exchanged threats. The healthcare plan didn't work out for you. I was disappointed as was most of America. What we have isn't working and we cannot seem to work together to solve the problem. Tax cuts are looming while football players sit, stand and kneel when the national anthem is played. Basketball players shout and protest and you yell at everybody. Maybe it is good that you get out your frustration and anger. We must find a way to solve all of these issues without tearing our country apart. You stir things up to a fever pitch. Are you mad or is there a method to your madness? I watch and listen and wish and pray and hope.

The leaves are turning. Maybe this discord is for just a season. Is my hope the real madness or is it that quiet wisdom that knows that living with hope is all that can save us?

HURRICANE

_____

October 18, 2017

Dear Donald,

I have not forgotten you, but I do feel guilty about how I have recently pulled away. After the Florida hurricane, I was swamped. I had to oversee all of the repairs to my condo following hurricane Irma. I had to remove the carpeting and gut the kitchen. The cabinets were soaked and made of a fiber board that would not dry out enough to prevent the possibility of mold. What a nightmare. I was relieved that it was not worse.

I just hired a management company to handle my condo because I am too busy to get down there. I decided to add to the insurance money to redo the entire kitchen, the bathrooms and upgrade the carpeting. The details were endless as I organized all of this from Cleveland using my rental agent, Home Depot and Serve Pro. The upgrades will glean a greater rental profit and the improvements will be a business deduction. I have learned this from you. I have been watching you for a long time!

You are running this country and doing a good job! I am sure you are looking out of the corner of your eye to check that your family is doing a good job with your companies. You jet all over the world and at the same time deal with praise from your fans and extreme scrutiny and criticism from your enemies. How do you do it? Your strength amazes me. You are inspiring. When I get stuck with a problem, I think of you and tell myself, "Yes I can."

I am usually awake at 5:45 in the morning. I make phone calls, get dressed, clean up and get to the pool by seven. An hour at the pool and then coffee and breakfast usually in a lot across the street from Dunkin' Donuts. Great Coffee. There, I meditate, pray, make more calls, review my day and build my courage. I run a few errands and then get to work on my magazine, sales meetings, radio show and keep tabs on my family. I don't spend much time with Dale, but we get along so well. It is a live and let live relationship.

I am avoiding telling you that I can't listen to the politics anymore. I have turned on Megan Kelly or Yoda just to hear light hearted banter void of debate and disgust. I really don't know how you tolerate it all. There is no relief, not even in sports. I spend my time listening to Christian radio and TV.

This political unrest is like living in an endless hurricane from which there is very little shelter. I am praying for you and the country, for myself and the future of my son and his family. I know you are praying too, Donald. You are so strong. Don't let them cut your hair. Like Samson, your strength may very well be embedded in your long hair. Many are irritated by it and it is the point of some bad jokes. It is bold and unique and is somehow a part of your power.

I love the Huckabee show on TBN. Thank you for supporting

his launch. The show is an eye in the storm. When I watch it, I smile from the minute it starts to the very end.

TELEVISION

October 22, 2017

Dear Donald,

Listening to the news stations is overwhelming. It used to be difficult for me to listen to the liberal stations bashing you and exaggerating every negative thing they could muster up, real or imagined! Lately, I am uncomfortable with the more conservative stations. I can't watch Law and Order because it is too cruel. I have to hope it is not based on reality. Are people really that crazy and mean?

Colleges have gone mad. Halloween is not fun anymore. People are using costumes to make political statements. Churches are not safe. My church which is beautifully diverse has hired a security guard. He walks the parking lot and roams in and out of the building during the service. I was told to lock my car doors and not to leave the building alone. Shopping centers are dying. This is sad, but the ones that are still vibrant scare me. They are targets for terrorism and magnets for unhealthy materialism. Tickets at sports arenas are ten times as expensive than they were when I was young. The arenas are vulnerable for protest and revolt. I can no longer relax in venues with large crowds.

Dale barely watches the news. He only watches college football and spends his spare time fishing and fixing stuff around the house. The man is happy. He laughs and smiles. I find myself staring at him marveling at how he has insulated himself from media overload, family drama and church politics.

I went to a church banquet after service today. Dale slept late and fed the birds. Feeding the birds is Dale's sacred moment. Catching fish on Lake Erie is a spiritual experience for him. While I am deeply concerned about the state of the world, he is counting the perch he has cleaned and has soaking in an old rusted pot.

I am watching a lot of Christian television. Some of the movies are corny, but the messages are wholesome. We need hopeful and decent programming that is filled with solid family values. I can relax when I watch Huckabee. It is a surprisingly refreshing show. I can breathe and feel like the world is intact and quite sane. I didn't love his show on FOX, but in an environment of Christian values, I am comforted and soothed by the program. I laugh a bit. I feel safe. Maybe I'll take up fishing. Good thing I didn't throw out that old pot.

BIRTHDAY

_____

November 12, 2017

Dear Donald,

Today, I am focused on two very important days, November 11th and 12th. My son was born on Veterans Day and has a heart for veterans. His father was born on November 12th. I am stunned that it is mid-November and it has been so long since I have written to you. I am still consumed with long distance renovating. Dale and I are flying to Florida again after Thanksgiving. We were just there a few weeks ago. After I returned from the last trip, I decided there will be no more tears over my condo. It is good to grieve a loss, but dangerous to live in this sort of grief.

My son's father passed away before he was able to see his first grandchild. That was over thirteen years ago. Now, there is a second, who he has not seen, at least from this earthly perspective. I would like to think that my late husband has the capacity to see all things from Heaven. Hopefully, he is watching over these two beautiful boys who sing "Happy Birthday" to their dad every year. Their mom, makes videos of the three of them. I revel in watching them from afar as I live in Ohio and they, in New York. It has been five or six of my birthdays ago that they moved. I will not let one more year go by without inventing some way to spend more time with them. You know, for the fun events, celebrations and experiences. They are coming to Cleveland to stay with me for Christmas. I will plan a spectacular week for them.

I think I am "aspirational." I heard that word on the news the other day as an announcer described the South Vietnamese citizens as being "aspirational." The announcer said they loved you because they were longing to be rich and successful, too. I can relate to that! I like you for a lot of reasons but aspiration, is definitely one of them. I aspire to accumulate more wealth because I don't feel that I have reached my potential.

Drawing from Melania, I wore very high heels to church today. Not as high as the pink ones she wore in China with that gorgeous oriental long dress with sleeves that looked like they were trimmed with pink mink. I am drawn to glamorous clothes, long hair and high heels. Have you noticed?

November 11th is the best day of my life. Having a son and grandsons are my greatest joys and achievements. Everything I try to do is for them. My son and his sons keep my heart pure and beating. I have watched you carefully. I know you adore your children and are drawn to glamour and success. But I think you are also drawn to more meaningful and soulful aspirations thanks to the miracles that our children have given birth in us. We bring them into the world and they bring us closer to God.

TAXES, SEX, ETC.

November 16, 2017

Dear Donald,

Sarah Huckabee Sanders is a star. I wasn't sure about her at first. She didn't seem old or powerful enough to take on the job of Press Secretary. She has earned my respect and admiration. I am impressed with her steadiness and confidence. She is unwavering in her comments and unmoved by the harassment of those who question her. Sarah is intensely supportive and respectful of you without being defensive. Fortunately, she can't be bullied or manipulated. From time to time, she even shares with viewers her charming sense of humor. She is her father's daughter and he continues to get my support and loyalty. He is always the calm voice in the storm. Sarah and her dad are solid, believable and decent.

After weeks of one news nightmare after another having to do with sex scandals, basketball players stealing sunglasses in China, more shootings, an earthquake and fighting over tax reform, I watch Sarah. Tax reform passed in the house today and she takes on the press with such class. She is calm. She is certain and not cynical. I want to be like her.

I continue to renovate my place in Florida. I am down to the details and it feels like an avalanche. That, along with my work here in Cleveland and staying connected to my Lebanese/ American tribe can be arresting. I know that you connect with everyone and still get all of the work done. Other leaders embrace these challenges and complete the course with such grit and grace. I try not to complain. I make lists and enjoy checking off my accomplishments.

I am still learning that success is possible if I embrace the mission that inspires me. I guess this goes for all of us. I have to let myself get excited about more than a plate of sugar. Some let drugs and alcohol derail them. Food is my drug of choice to distract myself from what has to get done. When I regain my thoughts, I brew a cup of tea and get back on track until it is time for lunch. I try to keep working until dinner when I remind myself to weigh and measure. I tell myself to stop and pray when I feel undone. I'll bet Sarah and Mike would tell me that I can do all things through Christ. I think their stardom comes from someplace sacred.

AWAKENING

November 18, 2017

Dear Donald,

What is happening to me? It is Saturday night and I am watching Vestal Goodman, the queen of gospel, singing at the Kennedy Center. She is not thin or gorgeous. She is carrying a handkerchief and wearing a long orange gown while she sings "God Bless America." She really means it. This sweet woman is being interviewed between her recorded performances. Did you know she was married in 1949? She sings with her husband who has a full head of snow-white hair and uses a cane. In my opinion they do not have wonderful voices. Good enough for Kennedy Center, I suppose. They are in love with Jesus and they shout in song that they believe Jesus is coming back.

Howard and Vestal Goodman are on Gaither TV. Howard said that his wife always had a small thin voice until a hurricane hit and blew away their home, which was a tent. He remarked that something came over her after that and she really began to sing loudly with strength and power. She received standing ovations

---

148

in theater after theater, performance after performance across the country. She often sang alone and sometimes with a church choir behind her. She always sang about Jesus.

Christian singers captivate me. When I watch them on TV they are never, in my opinion, beauties or sexy. Their clothes are of no interest to me. The singing is often loud and about the Lord. Just as I think they are a little crazy, I find myself mesmerized by their joy, sincerity and uncomplicated decency. While they are singing, they are connected to the Holy Spirit and in some way, I get connected too.

Howard Goodman is the only one alive of eight brothers. He talks about how sure he is that he will see his brothers in Heaven. No past, my friends, only future as he reminds us as he sings. In much music, God is found.

My cousin Laurie is sustained by her love of cooking, but mostly by her love of music. She hunts for music that lifts her spirit and takes her to a place of joy and gratitude. Laurie finds a hint of Heaven in these songs and singers. Since she believes in Heaven she can endure the disappointments here on earth. Filling her life with music has changed her taste of heaven into a feast. She lives in hope. She sings and is invincible.

I have endured a hurricane, and yet, I sing.

HAPPY NEW YEAR

January 6, 2018

Dear Donald,

It is almost the end of the first week of the new year. I haven't written to you in over a month. I was still repairing the hurricane damage to my property in Florida. When I returned to Cleveland, I had to rush to prepare for my family to come from New York for Christmas. I wrapped a huge gift, which my son assured me, would make me a hero. I try to make every visit special since I don't see my grandchildren very often. The gift was a big hit! My daughter-in-law is a very intense homemaker so I cleaned and cleaned and cleaned. I thought I covered everything, but I failed to clean out two coffee pots and there was mold inside of them. Ouch!

Donald, I learned something about myself, I was not embarrassed or upset about the moldy pots. I am a tremendously busy person and like everyone, I sometimes forget a detail or two. I have learned to cope with my oversights. I am proud that I accomplish so much. If there is an oversight, even with moldy coffee pots, so be it! It won't ruin my day.

I was more relaxed with my daughter-in-law because she is a super homemaker and so am I. We are both strong in different ways. I finally understand that and I think she does too. I was very complimentary and she was careful to contribute her skills while fully appreciating what I offered. At least we are not competing. We found win-win situations on that visit and that was great. It would be nice if the Republicans and Democrats could overlook a few things to find the win-win for our national government.

Donald, it is two degrees in Cleveland and it has been bitter cold for a few weeks. The sun is setting artfully, resting on the edges of the roof tops in the neighborhood. The snow looks so lovely against the sun's golden light at the end of the day.

The kids left today and I usually cry at their departure. This time I held myself together. I feel more secure about their love and not so dependent on their approval. There are some advantages to the end of the day. As darkness falls, there is a deep sense of quiet providing me the environment to ponder being older and wiser. If it is snowing, I do not long for the sun. If it is sunny, I don't forget the charms of winter. Florida and Ohio are such opposites in climate and they have taught me that both extremes are joyful.

Again, today, on the news I hear anti-Iran, anti-Israel, anti-American, pro-Democrat, anti-Democrat, bad Progressives, nasty Republicans and rational Republicans. Black beauty, black lives matter, white supremacy, uppity blacks, police are pigs but they are heroes in blue. Take a knee, don't take a knee, lose weight, take drugs, all kinds of legal drugs are at your fingertips, get insurance, buy, buy, buy car, a treadmill, jewelry, skin care, more and more and more while we feel that we have less and less to spend. I watch the news with one eye closed as I write.

There is sanity in my heart, but total insanity in the political world. I will turn it off for tonight and linger in the sweet reverie of my children at Christmas. I will remember my eight-year-old, Trey, sleeping in my arms and Lucas, his older brother, playing the piano by the Christmas tree. I would say, it was like a Norman Rockwell family Christmas. They have gone back home to their usual routines and I will return to mine. For now, I will remember all of the love that surrounded me.

THE BOOKS

_____

January 7, 2018

Dear Donald,

There is a new book out about you and everyone is talking about it on TV. No kidding. It is called Fire and Fury. It is creating an uproar and it is very critical and insulting to you and your family. Steve Bannon, who was involved with "eating" his words, may have put himself in a very bad position by raising questions about your fitness for office. Corey Lewandowsky supports you. But, the author Michael Wolfe, refers to you as crazy and unfit. The book suggests that you cannot read. I hope that is not true because one day, I want you to read my book and have the pleasure of reading the words of someone who views you in a positive, loving and respectful way.

Good for you for calling yourself smart and a genius. I am going to start describing myself that way, too. I am tired of my self-effacing ways. My kids are geniuses at seeing my faults and I have learned to laugh it off. I remind them of how amazing I am. They seem to wear glasses that highlight all of my faults and block my virtues. I have agonized over this, but you have taught me to toot my own horn, to myself. I don't have to toot it to the world, although, I am considering it.

Mike Pompeo, the CIA Director, has no patience for the exaggerated criticism thrown at you. Obviously, he likes and respects you. Finally, the resistant Republican politicians are beginning to step out in praise of all you have accomplished.

You are very different from former presidents and you are so confident about who you are. You do not cower to public opinion as you are true to yourself and bold in believing your good intentions. Carl Rove reports that he can't believe that Bannon has put himself in this terrible position. He thinks that Bannon's ego is beginning to backfire on him. Rove doesn't think you should have called yourself a "smart genius." What does he know? Rove is not the President. He is not a billionaire and has not accomplished anywhere near what you have. Who really cares what he thinks or has to say. Scripture states, "You shall know them by their fruits." Rove, a basket of apples. You, a tower of gold.

OPRAH

January 9, 2018

Dear Donald,

I was not thrilled, at first, with the notion of Oprah Winfrey running for president. It seemed a bit ridiculous to me. But then, I began to re-think it. She's a lot like you in some ways. No one can deny her extreme success and positive influence on women, blacks and humanity in general. I have done all of the things that she does in a very tiny way. I have had my own TV show and magazine. I have always taught and written about raising consciousness, increasing good will and kindness in the culture. I referred to my guests on my talk show as "pieces of stars, that had fallen from the heavens, to heal the earth"! In fact, before her shows turned in the direction of mental, physical and spiritual healing, I sent her copies of my show. In many ways, she is a soul sister.

Can she beat you in an election? I hope not. I approve of your presidency and the direction that it is going. I want you to stay in office for a second term. I know that both of us admire her

---

work, intention and success. I think that the two of you should work together and start a new political party. Something fresh, enlightened and healing to the awful divide that has become America.

The party should be called "American Dream" and it should be led by an equal presidential team...Oprah and Donald...both with equal power and status. Think of it, Presidents Oprah Winfrey and Donald Trump. The new party has to present a totally different approach to solving problems which is not contentious but based on common sense and consensus.

I like that neither of you has the need of financial gain. Both of you have a "call" from God to serve, transform and heal a country that is losing some of its magic, power and patriotism. There is the possibility in this union between the two of you. Women could claim their power and men could mature to a mass appreciation for the intelligence and empowerment of women. Leadership could be focused on raising the consciousness of the entire planet, while rebuilding the glory and beauty of the United States of America. We need roads, bridges, tunnels, super trains, spectacular housing and jobs. We can heal the great divides of race, religion, gender and politics if we can find a way for the two of you to work as a team.

I like that you are both real and not packaged to win votes. You are both succeeding in the utter truth of who you are. You are both authentically passionate about being agents of change.

Alabama defeated Georgia last night. Was one team really better than the other? Politics is not football. We need to take great minds and put them together to merge into a "United" States that work for liberty and justice for all. So, the two of you, unite. I think God may have a new way for Donald and Oprah to heal the land.

BILLIONAIRES

January 10, 2018

Dear Donald,

Shepard Smith on FOX NEWS doesn't seem to like you. He often has a snide "gotcha" tone to his voice and I find it unpleasant and disturbing. I long for objective reporting and sometimes I am just as uncomfortable with the news folks who clearly support you. I long to hear the facts of a story without the bias of broadcasters and news writers. There is very little of that on TV no matter what station I watch. Catherine Herridge is successful in remaining objective and stone-faced. She talks so fast and has so little facial expression, that often I can't follow what she is talking about.

Frequently, I turn to CNN, ABC, CBS, NBC, PUBLIC TELEVISION, TBN(Christian Broadcasting Network), FOX NEWS and FOX Business. I want to know what everyone has to say. Wolf Blitzer is consistently professional, but I don't want to watch him everyday. I often wince when watching most channels, they seem so biased. I generally support you, so FOX NEWS is the least painful. I am going to begin broadcasting on the Salem Radio Network. I am praying that I can be a voice of reason and inspiration.

This morning, I read in the news about a twenty-seven-year-old young man who, after he dropped out of Harvard, became the world's youngest billionaire. With his brother's help, he triumphed in Silicon Valley. Most men would likely say he is smart enough to run for Congress or the Senate. I am not sure it is all about being smart.

I don't think Oprah is taken seriously by men. Her wealth, charm, intelligence, courage, vision, enormous success in television, publishing, film production, acting and business is just not quite enough for the men I hear talking about her.

She is a full figured super feminine lady and I am not surprised that men are either threatened by her or unconscious about her potential. One would think that American men would be the most modern in such assessments. The truth is, that a "macho" spirit is still pretty strong here. A woman has a really difficult time leading the pack, no matter how brilliant or accomplished she might be.

I have noticed that I have plenty of reticence of my own, when it comes to taking seriously my accomplishments and potential. I am pushing to accomplish more, but I notice there is a part of me that is held back. I still question my destiny and wonder why I get no thrill from cooking? What kind of woman can't conquer her family with unforgettable cuisine? Darn, if Oprah hasn't mastered that as well! She not only loves to cook, but is touting recipes that are healthy, delicious and approved by Weight Watchers.

That woman can't do anything wrong. I almost hate to see her jump into a political war that will do everything it can to mangle her. Oprah's net worth is 2.8 billion dollars. Her presence is so strong that sharks will gather in packs to destroy her. I hope that she is indestructible. I want to be indestructible. If anyone can inspire me to be that, it is Oprah Winfrey.

MARTIN LUTHER KING, JR.

_____

January 12, 2018

Dear Donald,

Today, you are talking about love, God and the wonderful man, Dr. Martin Luther King. You are signing the necessary documents to honor him. Ben Carson is a breath of sanity, serenity and a calming spirit. I guess that comes from his mother and the stresses of the brilliant work he did as a pediatric neurosurgeon.

You, on the other hand, are a storm waiting to happen. Your fire and compassion are admirable, but I am concerned when you set yourself up as a target for the "haters." I know you are not crazy and you have little patience for political correctness. You say what you are thinking, no filters. I think you are passionate about honesty.

Your description about Haiti was pretty rough. Listening to the responses from the haters and supporters was painful for me. I dread each new negative comment about you. Maybe you believe that publicity is publicity, positive or negative. It seems to work for you. Donald Trump steals the stage on all of the stations. You are "out there."

Today, thank goodness, you were signing this completely non-racist proclamation. The television coverage was in stark contrast to yesterday's events. Ben Carson doesn't think you are a racist and I don't think so either. You are tough on yourself and hold others to your standards. You want to be generous and you don't want the American people to continue to be ripped off by the dealings of former Presidents.

The invitation on the Statue of Liberty reminds me that America is a remarkable nation. She has always welcomed the down-trodden so they might realize their highest hopes and dreams in this land of opportunity. We offer the "Golden Door" to those who want to come here to fulfill their potential and manifest their destiny. We have not demanded a guarantee of success. We compassionately accept immigrants and we always have. My father came to this country with nothing, as did many. He and others were models of citizenship building his life, assimilating into the American culture, having a business and providing employment opportunities, having a family and being a part of a community.

Please, choose your words carefully. Words are powerful. The part of America that voted you into the office of President wants you to succeed.

HAWAIIAN SCARE

———

January 13, 2018

Dear Donald,

It is snowing today in Cleveland. The sun is shining at Mar-a-Lago where you are happily golfing. Hawaii had a storm of sorts this morning. Cell phones lit up with a warning of a military attack with a twenty-minute advance to find appropriate shelter. Panic!!! It didn't take long for the powers at fault for this false alarm to correct the message. This has taken up air time on television and radio all the day long.

It has been over sixty years since these air raid warnings were broadcasted and then only as safety drills in schools. I recall that as students in school we would crouch under tables in cafeterias and desks in the classrooms with hands on our heads for protection. Really? This is going to protect people from a nuclear attack? I am sure that the films that were made of this procedure were used for propaganda in other countries. I don't remember being afraid because I knew it was just a drill. I did it impatiently waiting for it to be over. Today, we know that an attack can wipe out our country, civilization in the US as we know it. Whether it be a strike from a hostile country or a solar flare that hits our vulnerable grid, we are toast. Electronics won't work, cars won't start and the devastating trickle down from there.

Today, it wasn't a drill. For about an hour over a million people in Hawaii were alerted about a missile attack and were told, "This is not a drill." Some were covered with mattresses in bathtubs, others scurried to connect with loved ones. People couldn't believe it and stood in disbelief or resignation. They understood that if they were being attacked, no action would guarantee protection so why not just wait and watch. Then came the apology for the mistake. It was due to a shift change and doomsday was over without a scratch, physically. The residents were stunned, mad, anxious, frustrated confused and helpless. The fear lingered. The world watched.

There aren't any real defenses against this kind of attack. Innocents around the world are feeling defenseless. How can we calmly live in the midst of the unpredictable monster? Every day we realize the potential of military devastation on American soil and in countries around the world. Evil pops up randomly obliterating trust in the possibility of human transformation and positive evolution. How can the world know so much and be so collectively stupid?

Your base voted for you and hoped that because of the successes of your business life and family life that you could come up with an answer to end these threats. I know, they have been brewing for decades and now the world's "hot spots" are your problem. I am glad you aren't ignoring them and that you realize that quiet is not peace, it is just quiet.

GOLD MEDALS AND
AWARD-WINNING DRAMA

January 17, 2018

Dear Donald,

It was wonderful to watch Bob Dole receive the Congressional Medal of Honor for his service to our country. He is 94 and he and his lovely wife have so much to be proud of. I was glad to see that everyone lived up to the dignity of the moment. I was relieved.

Tonight is your fake news awards. You have been teasing about this for weeks. I am horrified but I will watch. This is not what we expect from our President. I am counting on you to use the event to your advantage. Each time I think you have gone too far, you amaze me by turning things around with no apologies. You are strong, and I am impressed with how impervious you are to the vitriolic criticisms.

New statistics are coming out about criminals and illegal immigrants. They are stunning. You are fiercely committed to your ideals and I await the next upheaval. Hurricanes, cold weather, forest fires and mudslides ought to be enough. But, even without them, there is a storm a minute in this administration. While you challenge the news media, you have made it more interesting. The entire country watches more than ever. It is the best soap opera in town with drama, passion, intrigue and celebrity. Politics is not dull at all, but fascinating and overflowing with surprises.

Your doctor shocked us all with a great bill of health for you. You say you don't sleep much and drink a lot of diet soda. You golf but you don't seem to do much else for exercise. You are healthier than most American men your age and a huge number who are much younger. Nothing about you makes sense or is predictable. You have everyone spinning about trying to interpret changing paces and volatile events of the day. I can hardly wait to find out what will happen next. I do cover my eyes from time to time, peeking between my fingers. Sometimes I am breathless with concern and excitement hiding under a pillow. This is quite a ride, as they say. There is one thing I am sure of. This story is eventful and life changing. I will not miss a minute of it.

STATE OF THE UNION

January 29, 2018

Dear Donald,

Tomorrow is the State of the Union Address. I am really looking forward to it. I tried to watch the Grammys last night but found it too painful. So much of the event had a political bent and it was shockingly negative about you. I had trouble with the evening and I really pushed to watch the red carpet, the first half hour of the show. Some of the work was brilliant, much of it was not. The fashion didn't appeal to me. It seems so pushed and overdone. I found myself wincing and regretful that I took the time to watch. I remember the first time I saw Lady GaGa with a slab of meat on her head at one of these award shows. Strange as it was, I even smiled. I have always loved her work. Why did it seem so overdone last night? I think the pervasive undertone of the political bias throughout the first part of the show was so off putting. I was not able to sit through the whole thing.

I turned to a series on PBS about Queen Victoria. The segment showed her understated ways as she struggled to adjust to the high fashion of the French. It was much more entertaining.

Have I become stodgy and closed minded? I question my reaction to the Grammys. I was angry and sad. I adore good music and have a broad appreciation for a great variety of music genres. I don't think it was the music, it was the tone of the show. They were mean, presumptuous and arrogant.

Donald, you were angry and passionate about your point of view when you ran for President. So many of us were shocked and relieved that someone, at last, was screaming "enough is enough" with regard to political correctness and sending our country down the river. You were reckless and maybe you could have spoken your truth a little more diplomatically. You were the voice for all of us who were too frightened to speak. The backlash is loud, ugly and frightening.

I always look for the silver lining. Here it is: Your truth is not the truth of your opposition, but it is for all who voted for you. Now the cards are on the table and there is an advantage to that. Unlike your opposition, I want to see and hear both sides. I want to build a wall and I want to build bridges.

MITCH MCCONNELL

———————

January 30, 2018

Dear Donald,

I watch the news each day to find out how you are doing. You are like family to me as you are to many Americans. I listened to Mitch McConnell and he surprised me. He seemed to like you. Thank you, Mitch for putting the divisions in our country into a different focus in your interview today. The media exaggerates and often voices opinions, not facts, into the news coverage. We see the events and listen. Everything is heightened with drama and condensed in a moment. As a country, we are on sensory overload and it is impacting our lives. We can't sleep, our relationships are suffering, we eat more or eat less from all of the stress. Our cortisol levels shoot skyward and this isn't good. Life in high definition, high speed, and high drama is not real. It is overly exaggerated, and our brains are on sensory overload. But maybe that is what sells.

My cousin went to visit her family at a vacation home in the Carolinas. She was amazed at the quiet and peaceful feeling of life without the news. Humanity has become inundated with the most intense moments of public life. We forget to experience life without the noise. Addictions to our screens and devices overwhelm us. Life in constant high speed is unhealthy. We live in a state of dread and panic. We have become numbed to the NEWS ALERT. At one time, we would rush to the television to find out the emergency. Now everything is in emergency mode and we continue to eat dinner through it all. We are psychically numbed. If we truly understood the gravity of the world news, we wouldn't be able to move. I have a TV in every room and I don't let a day go by without swallowing all of the drama of the news.

I live fairly close to the Amish in Ohio. I have visited friends there. The horse and buggies amble by in no hurry without the GPS or the Internet. There is no high fashion or high speed. Life is in slow motion and in some ways, it is utterly divine. I breathe in the smell of the blossoms in summer and the cold crisp air in winter. There is time for a family dinner blessed by an unhurried grace. I envy that way of life, but I could not live it. I can stop for a little while and cherish it. I can do a news fast and change the channel when I have reached sensory overload. I can read the classics and count my blessings. I can sing a glorious song.

GARBAGE TRUCK

January 31, 2018

Dear Donald,

There was another disaster today. Republican Congressmen, staffers and their spouses and families were on a train headed to West Virginia for a retreat at the Greenbriar Resort when the train hit a garbage truck. Several were rushed to the hospital and so far, one is dead. Fortunately, none of those traveling to the retreat were injured.

I felt like I was hit by a truck while watching the State of the Union Address last night. You did a great job of celebrating the successes of the past year, of reaching out to the "Dreamers," honoring heroes, parents, soldiers, children, remarkable citizens, police and patriots. I was so glad for the accomplishments of the year and grieve for the tragedies. I was not prepared for the childlike behavior of your opposition. It is simply disrespectful to you.

I tell you that I voted for John Kennedy, Bill Clinton and Al Gore. When I lived in NYC, I was a Democrat. After retiring, I moved back to Ohio, where I grew up. It took a while for me to get used to the thinking of the Midwest. I still have a bit of a liberal spirit. I think most people get more conservative as they age.

I remember what John Kennedy said, "Ask not what your country can do for you, but what you can do for your country." These words were a majestic inspiration that everyone could relate to. Democrats aren't like that anymore. If Kennedy were running today, he might be far enough to the right to be a Republican. Democrats today want the government to take care of everyone. I miss the self-reliant chant of the Democrats of my youth. I liked Regan. He bellowed, "Take down that wall." Bush 41 had to deal with Iraq and 43 had 9-11 on his slate. New York was never the same after that. Eventually, I left. I have not visited the site. Maybe I will do that this year.

Ohio is easy living for me. There is so much space and an abundance of affordable housing. The family values are intense, and the cost of living is reasonable. Life seems to roll at a slower pace. I think there are more churches and fewer country clubs. The sophistication is present, but relaxed. The pace is ambitious but there is time for family picnics. Ohio has a pro-worker and pioneer spirit. There is diversity here. One can eat around the world if you know where to look. Czech, Soul, Irish, Chinese, Japanese, German, Italian, Russian, Polish, Greek and the list goes on. It is all delicious. Even churches sell their homemade ethnic goodies as fundraisers. Homemade pierogi, garlic sausage made with fresh meat and garlic grown in someone's yard, bismarck's hot out of the oil, and baklava made with walnuts, not peanuts. Just to name a few of the delicacies. Delicious. Then there are the microbreweries that have become so popular. Some of these great restaurants will share a favorite recipe. I love it here.

I am on your side, my friend. How dare I call you that? We have never even spoken. You speak to me daily on TV. I laugh with you and cry for you. You are so strong, and I love it. I am so proud and glad to be an American.

VANESSA

February 12, 2018

Dear Donald,

I have been dreading this. Today, your daughter-in-law, Vanessa, received a letter that included what may have been a dangerous substance. As a precaution, she was taken to a local hospital. I am nervously awaiting an announcement that she is unharmed. I worry about your safety. Added to that, are concerns about Melania and Barron. There are so many disgruntled and crazy people in the world. You have such courage to take this presidency on when you could simply have been on the golf course. What is it with you? Is it ego, madness or profound patriotism?

Two Ohio police officers were shot yesterday. According to those who knew them, they were wonderful men and great cops. They were caring, professional, respected and loved. They were killed by a bad guy and all of the processions and tributes don't compensate for this heinous act. They responded to a 911 call. I am humbled and grateful by their dedication to public service. I don't want to give of myself as they did. I give in other ways, ways that don't require my life being at risk.

It has been two years now and I amaze myself for my willingness to part with a full ten percent of my income. I gladly give it to the church and charity. When I look at what these officers, the military and you risk, I feel stingy. I spent decades teaching and it was honorable work. I was proud of it, shaping the lives of children. I worked hard on producing and hosting consciousness raising television shows. After I moved to Cleveland, I published a magazine that empowered women in Ohio. I think all of my work has been reasonably noble. But I never intentionally put my life on the line. I guess I played it safe.

Where does the courage and commitment come from for that kind of ultimate sacrifice? Is it a calling? Is it a voice from God that overwhelms one's spirit? Is it a matter of feeling significant? Or, is it the need to be a hero?

I am called, and I listen. I am not called to that kind of danger. I bow to those who are. I am going to send flags and flowers, telegrams and prayers. I will take a moment of silence to praise and thank those who sacrifice so much. All of this is done for love of country and family, but mostly for a vast number of strangers, some who take freedom and safety for granted.

I hope there is a place for me in Heaven. For those who risk their lives for others, there is more than just a place, more than a Trump Tower, more than a palace. I hope there is a gold crown placed on the heads of those who sacrificed it all for another. I hope that these precious souls who were made perfect and holy in God's very own image, are enjoying God's presence and that they bathe in eternal peace and joy.

SPEAKING IN TONGUES

February 14, 2018

Dear Donald,

It is Valentine's Day. You have become a part of my most caring heart. When you, your family and Mike Pence are criticized, I am wounded and protective. And yet, I try to keep an open mind.

Joy Behar plunged into a negative and disrespectful response to Omarosa's (former aide of yours) comments about Mike Pence's way of praying. The vice president's effort to share with Omarosa his gift of praying in tongues was clearly misunderstood by Omarosa and Joy.

Diane, my cousin, called today. She couldn't understand why the women on The View would make fun of our Vice President talking to and hearing from God. She is a devout Christian along with her husband, Yarid. He has anointed me many times with holy oil when I was sick.

There are so many ways of praying in Christianity and in other religious traditions as well. Pence seems to be a devout Christian, a loyal husband and intensely moral. In his walk with Jesus, he, like millions of other Christians have been blessed with a special way of praying. He prays in tongues. It is called glossolalia. For those of us who have had that experience and treasure it, we immediately understand what Vice President Pence means when he says he is praying in the Spirit. He has a sense that he has not only spoken to God but that he has heard from God as well. Some experience this sacred connection by other spiritual disciplines.

In Charismatic churches, the sick come forward for healing during the service for a touch by praying hands. The recipients are often overcome with a profound feeling of grace which can render them limp. They are gently eased by ushers who embrace them as they faint to the ground and remain in a semi-trance for a period of time. When they are revived, they feel refreshed, blessed and touched by God.

We may not understand the mystery and magic of the mystical, but as long as the experiences are positive and loving, we ought to be open enough to listen to those who have had them, and respect them despite our own feelings. I have studied world religions. If the practices are hateful and violent, I reject them. If the traditions are helpful and healing, encourage kindness and compassion for others, I am patient enough to listen and learn.

Like Mike Pence, who by the way does not have a mental health issue, I will be praying in tongues today. I do every day and I know that my mysterious language will be eloquently translated to the heavens. The grace of God's wisdom and truth will be heard by me and fully understood.

FROM THE MOUTHS OF BABES

February 21, 2018

Dear Donald,

I am watching the students who gathered at the White House to talk with you regarding the shooting that occurred at a Florida high school this week. This a touching and remarkable sharing moment that is happening right now. Every comment from those who traveled from Parkland to talk to you about violence in our schools is wise and heartfelt.

The talk is about assault weapons, ages of those who should have guns, training, mental health, bullying, teacher training and on it goes. You are such a gracious president to listen and hear what these people are saying.

What I love most about the sharing of the teachers, students, parents and others is that the emphasis is constantly non-partisan. These kids are so grateful and honored to be able to share their ideas with you, face to face.

A grieving father laments that there is a security guard in the elevator at the White House, but there was not sufficient protection for his daughter at school. He buried his daughter and his railing and rage are piercing. You look like you are ready to cry listening to him. You are a daddy, you try to compose yourself. I am crying.

These children are emotional and heartbroken. A Sandy Hook mom is sharing. She had to bury her six-year-old. Thank God for these kids who gathered, organized and pushed to put an end to this. Thank God for you. They seem to understand that you are different and believe you will make a difference.

A surviving father shares how he lost a son at the Columbine shooting. He agrees with you, Donald, that we must create communities that are connected. We all need to change our hearts, connect with each other and learn to relate to each other no matter what. There should be no outcasts at school and nobody should have to eat lunch alone. This conversation points out that all of the division and ostracizing is literally killing our culture.

You know that gun violence is real. Your pain is real as you listen. I believe in you because I know you are listening to issues that many leaders before you have heard and cared about. What is it about you that makes me feel like the problem will be solved? You bring up the problem of a lack of mental institutions and that the city streets are overcrowded with the homeless. I interviewed many of the homeless on the streets when I did my television show in New York. Many were alcoholic and drug addicted in addition to being mentally ill.

We have mental issues in our country. We have drug and alcohol problems. There is a breakdown of families. We need jobs to come back to our country, which thanks to you, is happening. We need to start and end meetings and days with prayer. We have a country that has forgotten that we are one nation under God. Keep listening Donald, keep being you.

WHAT A DAY

February 28, 2018

Dear Donald,

The Reverend Billy Graham died a week ago at the age of 99. Today, his body arrived in Washington to lie in honor in the rotunda of the Capitol building. Such a lovely and sacred tribute for a holy and patriotic man.

He was called the "Pastor to the Presidents." He first met with President Harry Truman and offered prayer and support to many presidents on both sides of the aisle throughout the years. The former Presidents have made wonderful comments about him and how they will miss him. President Obama had conversations with him and you and Melania were with him on his birthday.

Many believed that Billy Graham was a special messenger from God. He came from humble beginnings growing up on a dairy farm in North Carolina. He had the opportunity to talk to millions of people not just in the US, but internationally. He held crusades across the country drawing countless to the love of Christ and became America's pastor. I learned that Billy Graham

---

received the Presidential Medal of Honor for his dedication to our country and to humanity. He was on the Gallup Poll sixty-one times, more than anyone else. He received honorary knighthood and received a star on the Hollywood Walk of Fame. He was truly a remarkable servant of God. It is no wonder he lies in honor in Washington. As a country, we will miss his presence and palpable love for all.

Later this afternoon, you met with many members of the Senate to discuss necessary steps to end school gun violence and gun violence in general. This was an action step that followed the Florida school shooting. The meeting was brilliant. I would expect nothing less of you. I watched with a sense of hope and relief that at last something will be done to end this. You shine at meetings like this. You lean to get action and you lean unafraid.

It has been an emotional week and a very touching day. I cave after eight hours of work. I want to be tireless like you. Maybe I should start drinking diet Coke.

RELIEF, JOHN BOLTON

March 22, 2018

Dear Donald,

Here it is, the middle of March and I can at last find the heart to write to you again. I was so relieved to learn that you appointed John Bolton as your National Security Advisor. I greatly admire him and he makes so much sense.

I agonize when stories about the alleged relationships with various women fill the news feed. I don't even want to talk to you about it right now. The news programs which are not on your side talk about your former trysts, non-stop. I can't bear to listen to it. The focus should be on issues of governing and the list of goals you have for our country.

It was on the news that Iceland eliminates all Down syndrome fetuses. In the US, ninety percent of all fetuses diagnosed with Down syndrome are aborted. Dr. Louden, a frequent commentator on FOX NEWS, has five children of her own and has adopted a child with Down syndrome. She says that her family agrees that Sam is a big bundle of joy. I love these stories.

The Loudens are wonderful people who demonstrate love and maturity.

Each day I fight to become a more decent and generous human being. I see you doing that. You are a man with a past, with a growing heart, with a vision for a country that has made many mistakes in its relatively short existence. You have a heart for the potential of this nation and for all of us who live in it and care about it.

I wonder how many brilliant citizens hold back their talents from serving the country they love because they can't forgive themselves for past mistakes. There are only a few saints on this planet. Even Jesus said, "Let the one who has not sinned throw the first stone." How many are suppressed and do not serve in public places because they fear the persecution of those stones that others will throw? Your courage in this regard is pretty remarkable.

I pray that with all of the temptations and tumult, you are able to hold your ground to serve your country. The author of the Book of Proverbs was not a saint, but a sinner who had much wisdom to share. He pressed on to follow God despite his sins. All of us need to push beyond our sins and save the world. By the mercy and grace of God, we can do it.

NORTH KOREA, EVERYWHERE

March 24, 2018

Dear Donald,

It has been nearly a month since I have written to you. The whole "Stormy Daniels" fiasco saddened me tremendously. Bringing this sort of scandal into the political discussion is dispiriting. There is a darkness about sexuality that haunts humankind. This force of nature, like all forces of nature, can be gorgeous, positive and miraculous. Our sexuality also has the potential to be evil in its power to seduce and betray. All are vulnerable to be seduced by drugs, alcohol, cigarettes, sugar, food, gambling, financial greed and lust. The devil will show you a darned good time, but he is a liar and when you least expect it, the good time turns on you and threatens to destroy your reputation, relationships, sense of safety, dignity and health. I pray for you and for all of us as lust, greed and gluttony lurk about stalking for an opportunity to spoil our destiny.

We must, fight against evil in all of its forms. You are blessed in that you are able to find your way over and over to better paths.

You forgive yourself and move on. I am very slow to forgive myself for my sins. I grovel and hide and berate myself endlessly for every flaw and digression from my concept of human perfection. If I eat a cookie that I shouldn't, I condemn myself to eternal damnation. I am not excusing sin, Donald, but in observing the way you forgive yourself over and over and stay standing and strong and brave and proud and blessed, I am in awe. Great men in the Bible were profound sinners before they turned to God. We do not just want to make America great again, we want to see our flawed selves as great again...redeemed.

Today the summit with North Korea was cancelled, we continue to struggle with school shootings, the Democrats and the Republicans have not found a way to work constructively together, and the gas prices are too high. On the other hand, you are keeping the door open for North Korean talks, hostages have come home, the country is working feverishly to solve the school shooting problem, the economy is strong, our embassy opened in Jerusalem and joblessness is at an all-time low in the US So many fear that the whole future of the world is dark and threatening, but you manage to make me believe that you are more than brave, more than a "giant killer." You are the win/win deal maker. You are not looking to conquer or connive, but to construct solutions where everyone at the table walks away a winner.

FOCUSED LIBERTARIAN

_____

April 3, 2018

Dear Donald,

I am encouraged today by the international movements toward Russia. I appreciate your positive influence on Saudi Arabia and your support of the Baltic States. You're leaning on China is to be admired as you try to improve international relations with North Korea. America is glad about your relentless and bold support of Israel and your firm stand for compliance with regard to the deal made by the Obama administration in Iran. I am still unhappy about Syria and wish you could do more, but I like what you are doing at the southern border. If necessary, you are willing to call on our National Guard and help from Mexico to halt the onslaught of Hondurans marching toward the US. I also like your success with ISIS. You are being very compassionate about the "Dreamers."

I am relieved that you are still so ambitions creating and recreating your cabinet. I really love that you are working well with John Bolton. It does frighten me that you are taking on

Amazon, Facebook and Apple. They are so huge that I fear they will swallow you. China is huge. Some of these world leaders stay in power for so long that I feel they have an advantage over you. What am I thinking? You are fearless. You always end up on top. Your courage is commendable. You are Donald J. Trump!

I love that companies are coming back home. Your mantra is "let's talk" and you keep your door open to welcome dialogue. You have stood up against sanctuary cities and at last, those in California who were afraid to take this on have found their courage and are standing against this mismanagement of immigrants.

We helped to rebuild China and it is time for us to demand fair trade. I trust you in the midst of all of this craziness. This is when you thrive. I was a teacher and so "report cards" are my thing. You were in Richfield, Ohio last week and I was heartbroken that I couldn't get there to see you. I would have handed you your report card in person. You would certainly be on my Honor Roll! I would write on it, keep up the good work Donald. EXCELLENT. OUTSTANDING. You are most likely to succeed.

CALIFORNIA

June 6, 2018

Dear Donald,

There is good news for Republicans in California this morning. The so called "blue wave" is not what was predicted. I agonize about the imperfections and problems on the Republican side. I continue to support the need for immigration reform and getting people off of welfare and working. These "investigations" against you are aimed at bringing you down while ignoring the wrong doings of the Democrats. The obstruction and resistance are historic and destructive.

Where is Melania? I know that she had surgery, but her visual absence is disturbing. I feel for her. She is not enjoying any positive press. Your enemies are obsessed with making you and Melania look as bad as possible no matter what good you may be doing for the country. As lovely as she is, the press spends very little time praising or admiring her. Keep being strong for us. Both sides have their issues.

Like Melania, I hate the bullying. It is never appropriate but especially not in government, schools or communities. You, Donald, set this tone. So many of us were as upset and angry as you were about many issues, but we were afraid to speak up. You took it on. You were not politically correct. All the anger on both sides of the fence terrifies me, but I think it is better that folks are expressing it, short of violence. Americans need to voice their feelings to be understood. Many of my New York friends and family have different political views from mine but we love one another and we don't fight.

I was in New York for five days. I stopped writing this on June 6, and just got back to Ohio on the 11th, very late in the afternoon. Everyone is buzzing about North Korea and I have the strangest feeling that it is going to be OK. The entire world is watching Singapore and waiting with a hope that the summit will lead to good news for all.

I feel strangely safer than I have in a long time. I think the noise about trade wars is going to die down too. The level playing field will ultimately be good for everyone. Keeping the Congress in Washington to prevent the government from moving forward to solve its budget problems is a good move.

This no-nonsense approach is appealing to me. Everywhere I go I see help wanted signs. That is a good thing. Strength, common sense and clear and fast action are a part of your DNA. I remain fascinated and encouraged by your unique and controversial style.

CENTRAL AMERICA

———

June 14, 2018

Dear Donald,

I enjoyed listening to former Secretary of Homeland Security, Jeh Johnson. His comments were clear and helped me to understand what was going on at the border. What I appreciated so much was that he prefaced his comments with a statement that he was not going to take a Democrat or Republican stand on this issue. He was quite open about the huge problems in Central America. The seemingly endless flooding of thousands of families and unaccompanied children over our border is not about to change in the near future.

I pictured thousands of families swarming my pretty house, climbing over the railings and roof, begging, lonely, angry, hungry, thirsty, and dirty. I am heartsick when my adult son ever goes through a period of struggle. For example, when he must face a job change, change of residence or an issue with one of his precious sons. He has what we call "champagne problems." His

———

problems are where his family should live or if the kids take tennis lessons or go to baseball camp.

The immigrants from Central America are coming from terrible conditions and are risking their lives to get here. Parents are sending their children because they cannot give them the future that they might have if they can make it in America, the "land of milk and honey."

My father left his father in Lebanon nearly a century ago. Dad was 18. He never saw his father again. The lure of the promise of America was intoxicating to him. My father came here legally. He was excited and anxious, but not desperate. Desperate people are not stopped by laws if they can break them and possibly get away with it.

I would like to see a twenty-point plan to toughen the border and transform the tragedy of the economic breakdown in Central America. Mexico, Belize, Costa Rica and Panama need to help. We need a wall. Consensus between parties, better facilities, efficient laws and deportation methods are absolutely necessary. The US must not enable the other countries in their manipulative practices of pushing their unwanted on us. Our "Golden Door" was hard won. Other countries must do the hard work of building free and prosperous countries in their own lands.

FBI - CLINTON

June 18, 2018

Dear Donald,

I am listening to the Clinton email probe report and Mr. Grassley's comments on the FBI response to the destruction of emails, the comments of Michael Horowitz and the current leader of the FBI. Diane Feinstein is ignoring the total Clinton fiasco.

The endless investigations concerning you are exhausting and infuriating. The legal process is too long and the discussions and incriminations are numerous on both sides of the aisle. Orin Hatch, a Republican senator from Utah is confronting the conclusions of the report. He sees so much bias revealed in the report and wonders why the FBI is not being held accountable. Christopher Wray, FBI leader, is standing up for the majority of the members of the FBI. Where do we go from here? Christopher Wray lists a multitude of corrective actions, but it all sounds like a lot of bad folks are getting off the hook.

Leaks, unauthorized contacts, violations of policy at the FBI were overwhelming. Christopher Wray is reorganizing but seems

---

to be suggesting that from now on we will do better. Democrat Patrick Leahy says that the FBI tainted Hillary Clinton's election while the Republicans argue that the FBI shielded her and did what it could to sabotage you.

Wray concludes that Mueller is not on a witch hunt. John Cornyn, Republican senator from Texas, seems to support that but clearly feels that Comey, and a large number of FBI agents, are so biased and unprofessional that in addition to firing Comey, a purging of a very large number of agents may be necessary in addition to a training overhaul.

While I am impatient with this process, I know only too well that good relationships do not just happen without a tremendous amount of thought, discussion and an endless examination of ideas. I am taking a deep breath here and supporting all the investigations that it takes to uncover mistakes, craft better practices and principles, and make America great again.

HEARTBROKEN

_____

June 20, 2018

Dear Donald,

I am heartbroken for everyone and everything that is going on at the border. The workers have to be exhausted managing the tremendous overflow of applicants, women, families, abusive cartels and huge shipments of illegal drugs. Then, there are the children who came without parents. They are desperate and longing for what we have in the United States. They may not qualify for asylum, but they ache for it with their hearts.

I am heartbroken for you. I know deep inside of me that you honor children. You have honored your own children and they honor you. I know that you want to protect all of the children in the world and are doing all that you can to establish a strong border to protect our homeland. "Charity begins at home." We have nothing to give if we lose our strength as a nation. To be a nation, borders are necessary. I know that you want a solution for the Dreamers, and that you want solutions at the border. What is the answer? More judges? More facilities to house the masses that beg to get in legally and illegally? Better laws? Clearer laws? We have inspired and supported an end to an enormous amount of world poverty. This is a good thing. When does giving become enabling? You and I both know what it means to be an enabler as we have suffered watching family members weakened by the so called "do gooders." When is enough, enough? How do you sort out the difference between helping, protecting and dangerous enabling?

You have done so much good and I know that you will help this issue at the border as well. You have engineered the biggest tax cut in history and that has done a remarkable thing for business. The market is soaring, and jobs are abundantly available. Unemployment is at its lowest in 44 years, African Americans and the Hispanic community are enjoying the benefits of jobs. Women have the lowest levels of unemployment in 21 years. MS13 members are being deported by the thousands. Chrysler is back from Mexico and moving to Michigan along with a plethora of other huge companies returning to the US and bringing enormous amounts of money with them to invest into this country. Politicians are throwing biblical quotes around in an effort to make you look "evil."

I know that any man who can invent THE SPACE FORCE cannot only believe in the biblical promise that, "All things are possible," but can and will find a way to solve this impossible problem at the border.

THE CHILDREN

June 26, 2018

Dear Donald,

Families being separated at the border is a mess! Other administrations had to deal with it and it was a mess for them too. I wonder why the people from the previous administrations are not able to share with you all the problems that go along with separating children from their parents. What do we do with this unmanaged problem? We manage it. These people are not going to stop coming and so, until we can change the laws, we need to reorganize the way we function at the border. I know that you are doing your best to stop the madness and at the same time, not be abused and used by illegal immigrants.

These children are helpless. Their parents took huge risks to come here with them. I support addressing the problems in their homelands, but we cannot solve all the problems in the world and we cannot let everyone come here illegally. Political asylum is very likely warranted for many of them. This situation has been a problem for former presidents. I am moved by the fact that former

Republican President Bush has become a close friend of former President Bill Clinton. Presidents should convene frequently to share experience, strength and hope. That's how "twelve steppers" do it in Alcoholics Anonymous. They share a common problem and support one another in finding a solution.

If you can start a Space Force, you can start a "President's Council" where living former presidents gather in a dignified and supportive manner to share ideas. I am grateful that the former presidents are respectful of one another and of you, as well. It is difficult for them as they often do not like what you do and say, I am sure. I see you restraining yourself as well, as you should, when it comes to talking about our former presidents.

Instead of competing with one another, these great leaders could combine, consult, co-operate, co-ordinate, care, come together and share their wisdom to support solutions and public good will. This is the way we are "One Nation, Under God."

BABIES, OURS AND THEIRS

June 29, 2018

Dear Donald,

Nothing pulls harder on our heart strings than children in peril. You have quickly moved to reunite parents with their children from whom they were separated at the border. Women rage in protest against a Supreme Court judge who might threaten Roe v. Wade. I wonder at the irony of this. Surely some concessions can be made for unborn children who are alive and well in the womb. How fully alive and well do they have to be? Can we rethink that parameter?

I am sweating and shaking as I type this. This is up close and personal as I painfully recall my reckless youth. It is easy to moralize on a high horse now that I am older and not fighting raging hormones. It is easy to forget that the "make love, not war" movement encouraged love fests, free love and sex without borders. In retrospect, this was all to our detriment as a society. Decades later, we are a nation confused about family values and busy redefining our roles and priorities. The world is in "future

----

shock," too much change in a short period of time. It has happened so quickly and radically that our entire perspective is re-focused minute by minute.

Americans are certain about some important things. We do not want to terrify children. We want to secure our borders in the most humane way possible, reining in the abuses of abortion rights. The practice has been pushed to a level that has made many of us uncomfortable, no matter how liberal we may be. I have interviewed many women who profoundly grieve their choices to abort their children and profoundly regret much of their sexual behavior. Is it time for us to re-think our moral compass? Sex is a very complicated issue and every sexual decision is accompanied by a myriad of complex consequences, good and bad.

When I retired last night, I grieved these issues. Many took to the streets today wailing for rights, freedom and protection of children. But what of the unborn children? I wonder. Were they murdered in the womb, but now alive and waiting for us in Heaven? What don't we know? Can we slow down and rethink our choices, values, egos, lusts and morality? We sing, "God Bless America!" Can we slow down and ask ourselves at every turn, what are we doing that God would bless?

TARIFFS AND TEARS

July 2, 2018

Dear Donald,

You always seem calm, confident and aggressive. At the same time, you are reassuring and optimistic about tariffs and the border. The entire world seems angry with us regarding the tariffs that you are placing on them. You insist that the entire world has been taking advantage of us for a very long time. They charge us huge tariffs and flood our borders with illegal immigrants. One tearful mother embraced her seven-year-old daughter with whom she was reunited today. She told those who might want to come to the US to go to another country as the people here are heartless.

I know that we are a people of great heart and generosity. This is why millions fight their way to the borders to get in. We have not been perfect at the border, but we have been patient and diligent in working out the overwhelming problems there.

I am forcing myself to listen to news on all of the various channels and making an effort to keep an open mind. I have voted as a Democrat and as a Republican and I am not comfortable with defining myself as one or the other. I also watch films which present various points of view. It is important that we keep our minds courageously open. Some of the actors you have insulted are, in my opinion, great talents. At the same time, I have not agreed with their reactions to you. Often, I feel like there are no adults in the room.

I am tired. You are tireless. I want someone to tell me that you are human. Do you ever just crawl under the covers long before bed time and moan, "Enough!" On your mind you must have tariffs, the border, the Supreme Court, North Korea and the long list of world leaders who seem angry with you. Yet, you swear that they are calling and asking to make a deal. None of this phases you. They all want to make a deal and you want to make a deal with all of them.

In the meantime, I am tired for you. I will take to my bed and moan while you continue to take on the world.

CHILDREN IN A CAVE

July 4, 2018

Dear Donald,

Today I am trapped, like Thai children in a cave. What if my leader has misled me? I am like the young boys in Thailand, trusting my coach who I am sure meant well. I see so much dissent in the government on both sides of the aisle that it is difficult to trust anyone. Every day, I have to listen, learn, watch, think and make decisions about how to vote, who to trust and what to do with my money and my time. Everyday there is the possibility that I will make the wrong choice and I will be trapped in a "cave" with no guaranteed safe way out. Worse than that, my children or grandchildren could be lost or trapped and what if they were not found and I could not help them?

I was in Thailand many years ago and I was sitting on an elephant and curiously riding up a mountain waving to little village children gathered in the distance. The skies were blue, and the sun was warm. The trained and quiet elephant would carry me up and later down the mountain. I would, in the balmy evening, enjoy an elegant dinner at a glamorous hotel in Bangkok. My husband, on the same evening, would be entertaining troops. He was booked in top night clubs in the Far East for months.

I ponder the dozens of incidents that might have ended in injury or harm or dire circumstances. I traveled unwittingly to dangerous parts of the city to purchase fine silks and beaded dresses. Young children no older than six or seven combed the streets at night selling marijuana in coffee cans. The finest dinner clubs housed, in rooms with glass picture windows, gorgeous women who waited to be chosen by male patrons for an evening's pleasure.

I don't know why I am so afraid today. It is Independence Day and the sun is shining. I am invited to a lovely poolside party at 3:00 and many good friends will attend. The food will be opulent and the house is gorgeously set on acres of green pastures. Denise may show us her horses. Frank will be proud of his new spectacular pool. My children in New York will go to a barbecue with dear friends and tomorrow will head to Montauk for a week's vacation on the beach.

All is basically well, but I am in tears and my shoulder is tight and aching. My heart is with the children in Thailand who are trapped in a cave. The arduous task of planning their perilous rescue weighs heavily on my heart. I worry about them. I worry about you and Melania and the Democrats, Congress and the FBI. Of course, I can't forget about Cleveland losing LeBron James.

I am living in America. By the hundreds of thousands, immigrants beg to come in. All is well, but I am afraid. At any given moment, my leaders could lead me into a dark and deadly cave.

Pray with me Donald. Pray for the children who are lost. Pray that God will bless America.

CAPITOL HILL

———

Dear Donald,

I am jealous of your brave curiosity and involvement in national politics and International affairs. You've watched and studied it for a long time from a position of the "street" so to speak. Are you taking some clandestine miracle drug that keeps your mind going without ceasing and your energy level at high levels for hours beyond what is normal for most of us?

Are you watching what is going on at Capitol Hill today with congressional hearings involving Strzok and his hateful emails? This is painful to watch. There is a level of contention that I find overwhelming. Added to what is going on at this hearing, which I am sure you will hear at some time, you are dealing this week with NATO, Germany, Britain, The Queen and Russia. You are traveling all over the world! You are attending functions from early morning to late evening. You are discussing many global issues. You look so relaxed and confident. You are standing firmly against others in every meeting. You seem unruffled.

———

I, on the other hand, am working on finding a new publisher for my magazine. This is exhausting. I am transitioning from the old publisher to a new one, dealing with other local publishers who are undermining me, catching up on hurricane damage repairs at my condo in Florida, putting two major radio interviews together and financing the copy editing of my first finished book. This week, the Florida air conditioner malfunctioned, the Cleveland garage door broke down, the insurance company refused to cover obvious hail damage to the roof here and the price of gas and print are skyrocketing.

While you calmly jet, my cousin, Laurie, has not listened to the news in a week. Her husband has been in a hospital in Houston where he was rushed while traveling from a family vacation. She was afraid to let anyone at the hospital know her political affiliation. Her husband's medical condition was critical and she feared some nurse, worker or doctor might subconsciously (or consciously) undermine a positive outcome for a patient whose political preference did not mirror that of the medical professional. She kept the television news off and carefully censored her speech.

You have arrived at Churchill's castle for an elegant welcoming ceremony hosted by the Queen. Melania is all in yellow and gorgeous. There is a royal guard, trumpets, tuxes, bag pipes and gowns. NATO was a success.

The senate is in a free and spirited debate, but it is not a bloody battle. Daytime debates rage on in the US Congress, but Europe has paused and is watching the British roll out the red carpet as only they can. A contentious day ends with the royal treatment. All in a day's work.

HELSINKI

_____

July 15, 2018

Dear Donald,

I have never paid so much attention to political meetings as I have since you have become the President. I am glued to the screen as you and Melania arrive in Helsinki. I had to really hunt into my memory bank to remember exactly what country Helsinki was in. It is in Finland, of course, and I watch in wonder as I note that the global fashion look, as I get older, is more and more similar. National folk costumes, although revered, are not the fashion statement of the day. The modern day fashion look across the globe has become homogenized.

Are we all more alike in every way across the globe? We are starting to look more alike. A hundred years from now we might all be more of the same color and might all speak the same language. We might all know how to control our tempers, organize our resources to eliminate poverty everywhere and work together to control the universe.

I am the "silver lining" queen, always waiting for and expecting miracles. The skies are blue in Helsinki and the people greeting the President as he deplanes there, are smiling, kind and welcoming. For a few moments, I can breathe, relax and believe that everything is just fine in the world. Watching the contentious members of Congress insult one another this week made me sad, mad and afraid.

President George W. Bush, years ago, said of Vladimir Putin, "I looked into his eyes and saw his soul!" You, Donald, send a positive message in your "Trumpian" way. "We'll see," you say. Your message is basically, "Heck, what is there to lose? Isn't it better to meet and try to make a deal?" You got fourteen billion dollars for NATO by wheeling and dealing in your unique and unorthodox political style.

Are Putin and Kim playing you? You have been tougher than former leaders but while you do that, you seem to smooth talk your way into negotiations. Some compare Putin to Stalin. Some compare you to Hitler. Listening to such comparisons flying around can make us all teary and fearful.

Sometimes I envy those who are oblivious, because their ignorance is indeed bliss compared to the shock waves televised to those who are brave enough or foolish enough to watch.

THE RUSSIANS ARE COMING

————————

July 16, 2018

Dear Donald,

You are shocking, yet again. The world expected you to publicly chastise Putin in your sit down today for meddling in our elections. Instead, you chastised the Democrats and Hillary Clinton. Putin was open to having all the Russians accused, questioned according to Russian Law with Robert Mueller and the FBI team present. He invited them all to Russia. You listened. Such an outrageous invitation has never been extended before.

You are busy deciding what kind of a deal you will make. What is your strategy? You have not made that clear. Both Democrats and Republicans were not happy with your performance today. I am ducking, my friend. You are going to get a ton of criticism for being too easy on this "bad guy." People on both sides of the aisle see Russia as a Big, Bad Wolf.

What they don't see, is what you have up your sleeve. You were so blunt with all the members of NATO. Every country was held accountable for their offenses. What I know about you is that one of your strategies is "the iron fist with the velvet glove." I am not buying that you are not or will not be tough enough on Russia. You have decided to wheel and deal and step by step you will do that. You will hold your line, but you have clearly chosen a different tone with Putin than you have with Kim or Assad. I am going to reserve judgment here. You don't trust the FBI at all. When they are involved in reporting conclusions about voting interference, or anything at all right now, you are holding back an opinion. I don't think you trust Putin either, but you are treading softly. He is throwing you the "World Cup" ball. What he surely must know is that you are "carrying a big stick."

SPEAK SOFTLY / BIG STICK

————————

July 17, 2018

Dear Donald,

I was astounded at your persona with Putin yesterday as was the entire world. You were so kind, accommodating and gentle that I felt you were dealing with an injured puppy and not an evil snake. The forty-four billion dollars this year and hundreds of billions of dollars in the coming years that you have insured for NATO by standing up to our European partners will be powerful against the Russian aggression. You were shown great respect by every leader around the world. The bad guys, for example, the leaders of China, North Korea and Russia wind up looking like your best friends. The optics are stunning and the message is confusing.

You are creating a more powerful military than we have ever had in the United States You have confidently and firmly faced up to Iran, North Korea, China, NATO, the possible corruption at the FBI and the actions of Russia in Syria. Your actions are commendable. Your personality is both priceless and perilous. I have a love/hate relationship with your style as so many of your supporters do. You are likable and terrifying at the same time as your political style is unprecedented and at times astonishing.

Peace through strength is achieved with a strong military and a strong economy. You have achieved both. You hunted through the transcripts of your remarks to Putin and realized that you used the word "would" instead of "wouldn't," quite by accident. Action speaks louder than words my friend. The world knows what you have done. You have stood very firmly against the improper actions of Russia.

The public wonders why you waited so long to clear this word confusion up? I don't blame you for waiting to respond to the critics. Often, I need time in my own dealings to rethink events and comments that I have made. Will this situation damage your status in future elections? I don't think so. Cream rises to the top. You are the real thing, I think.

It is my birthday today. I should be sick and old, but I am not. I am beating the odds my friend, and so are you. When I blow out my candles tonight and make my wishes, one of them will be that Divine guidance will be abundantly yours this year and in years to come.

COURT, KIDS AND THE FBI

———————

July 18, 2018

Dear Donald,

I often feel teary while watching the news. Maxine Waters terrified me with her anger and yelling at Democrats, urging them to close in, scream at and intimidate Republicans in every public place. The truth is that most Americans have some leanings in both liberal and conservative directions. Most of us would not bully others in public places, but it only takes a few to create havoc. Maxine Waters incites a dangerous level of fury which could lead to tragic violence.

The Republican members of Congress are furious about being stonewalled by the FBI and Trey Gowdy is raging about it. Turns out, among other redactions in discovery, there was a seventy-thousand-dollar expense for a conference table for the FBI. That bit of information, along with shocking degrees of hate and disgust for you on the part of FBI members who were in charge of investigations, was disturbing. It doesn't seem possible that any degree of fairness or impartiality could be possible in an investigation run by enemies of our president.

The kids who have been separated from their parents are a sad story and Melania brings some compassion to the forefront. The issue is extremely complex and the solutions will take swift and bold actions and changes in the law. This entire mess is clearly a problem that has been going on for decades and you are confronting it and demanding a solution. Immigration has become chaotic and a threat to everyone involved.

The Supreme Court is about to change as one judge hands in his resignation and you are sure to replace him with a conservative pick. Other Supreme Court liberal judges are also getting up in years, and as they leave, you, the president, will have an opportunity to hand pick more conservative members.

CNN was dreary and depressed when I tuned in yesterday. I force myself to watch it even though I often find it unfair and unreasonable. They hopelessly put their heads together looking for a way to stop the "red wave." It is gaining momentum. I am rooting for it, but at the same time, I am searching my soul to see what I can do to build bridges across the aisle. Threats to harm one another are off of my grid.

I pray that we are not so much red or blue but remember that we are one nation under God. If indeed we all agree that, "In God we Trust," then we need to pause and pray for a peaceful path forward.

MY SON, MY SON

_____

August 2, 2018

Dear Donald,

There are so many things going on at once. Never have I seen so much focus on politics and a presidential election as I have in the last few years. This morning, my son and I talked on the phone for nearly an hour about all that is going on in your administration.

Not far from his home, in the last week, there was an MS13 murder. Like me, my son has a myriad of political opinions, some liberal, some conservative and some a little of both. The country is redefining what it means to be a Democrat, a Republican, a Progressive or a Socialist. What excited me the most was that my son and I were having a spirited and interesting conversation about politics, morals, abortion, ideas, raising children, immigration, suppression of ideas and free expression, what kids are being taught in schools and how much we are grateful for the power of our vote.

You have a talent for keeping the news not just focused but obsessed with all that is going on in the administration. I have never experienced this kind of mass attention to politics. While a lot of us may be upset by the hundreds of issues being discussed, I know that so many of us are more engaged in thought and discussion about what we think is good for the country than we have ever been. I am learning about Russia, NATO, Israel, Iran, China, Japan, North Korea, South Korea, the Korean War, Congress, the Constitution, The Supreme Court, The FBI and a myriad of other things that I have never been so interested in and aware of before.

Our mother/son conversations have never been this spirited. Right or wrong, you make us think, evaluate, research and compare notes. There are at least three generations to consider. I am concerned about my grandchildren who feel the pressure of extreme liberal thinking in New York schools. I am concerned about parents who want only the best for their children and receive so many confusing messages that they need to sort out. I am concerned for the grandparents who want to guide, but do not want to alienate their precious young ones.

You make us mad, glad, make us listen and get engaged. As Americans, we are interested, excited and passionate. Conversations happen with one another about ideas and philosophies. This is not like anything I have ever seen in politics. Good or bad, right or wrong, you are waking us up. People think profoundly and thoughtfully about what is important to our country and how we are going to get it. Like never before, I deeply cherish the right to vote and the thrill of deep and engaging political conversations with my son.

SUMMER INSPIRATION

August 6, 2018

Dear Donald,

You keep me going. No kidding. I am doing ten things at once! I have several books in process, a radio show which has stalled, a possible podcast in production, a Florida condo that I must keep rented, keeping my house in Cleveland in order, the magazine that I own and publish which I sold, my relationship with my significant other of nearly fifteen years, my obsessive calls to my adult son and his children, my extended family obligations to the Lebanese tribe that I am a part of in Cleveland along with Dale's family in Columbus and California and my son's extended family in New York, my cousin Laurie in Florida and my best friend, Stuart on Long Island who is nearly as crazy as I am. Stuart can't sleep.

I won't tell you why Stuart can't sleep because it wouldn't be fair to Stuart. It's nobody's business. I will say that it works in my favor because he is usually available to talk to me and listen to my woes and wailing. I have added to this long list, an obsession with exercising at the local pool four days a week and working out at the gym afterwards.

With all of this going on, I feel useless. I feel that I am not enough. My sister, Shirley, at least cooks. She feeds people, lots of people. They love it. Dale fixes everything. He rides around town in his white truck and all the folks who have had their fancy houses built by the high-end builder that Dale works for, run to the curb like Dale is the ice cream man. They can't wait to get his advice about the fancy faults in their fancy houses. Stuart is a retired doctor and still gives a lot of medical opinions to all of his ailing friends. Stuart has many friends and they are all ailing. My children are very busy and wish I would not FaceTime so much. There are too many people in my tribe and I am invited to a wedding, shower, birthday, funeral, dinner party, picnic, church gathering, baptism, going away party, coming home party, and holiday party a minute. It is exhausting, and I am so annoyed with myself.

I want to be you, Donald. You run in circles, up and down and in and out of jets and helicopters and stadiums and the Whitehouse and palaces and summits and global meetings. You are on twitter and television and radio...a sound bite a minute. You have a mission that you have embraced with a passion that is unstoppable and impervious to criticism. You make me believe that no matter how crazy I am, that maybe, just maybe I am not crazy. Maybe I am a fighter. Maybe I am someone who never gives up. I'm cooking the only way I know how to and fixing the world one typed letter at a time. I'm rooting for you and making sure a lot of others are too. I am the gift of "inspiration." I am enough.

GOOD NEWS, BAD NEWS

August 10, 2018

Dear Donald,

Today it is bad news. I hate it! The elections across the country went fairly well for Republicans and that was good. The Republican turnout needs to be stronger. That was bad. The Manafort trial is a nightmare. Was he in trouble with money and the Russians and was he trying to maneuver you to get some leverage to get out of his own trouble? How would I know? I'm just an observer, trying to make sense of it all. My Aunt Helen used to babysit me when I was a little girl and she loved soap operas. This day of news reminded me of her favorite show, As the World Turns. It was a drama disaster a minute.

After the Manafort trial coverage, the stories trending were discouraging. North Korea is being true to form. Kim wants a world with a ribbon around it for its concessions. So far, they have not been nearly enough to satisfy your agreement. It is good that they returned some remains of our soldiers of Korean War, they have not been shooting missiles and some hostages were returned without giving them any money. These were acts in good faith, but the real goal of denuclearization is not happening, yet. Bolton is not happy. I never thought he would be. He draws a hard line.

Omarosa is a problem. I knew that she would be. I felt something scary there when I was watching her on Say Yes To The Dress. I know that is crazy. I don't know much about her and I will read her book, but don't discount my "feeling." I felt trouble and dread while watching her and some sense of worry about her involvement with the campaign and the White House.

Dale went fishing today. He is not complicated like you, Donald. My guy is middle America and blue collar. He is a lot smarter that he thinks he is. He gathers tremendous information listening and watching. He is a man of few words, but a considerable amount of basic wisdom. He is at peace with slow and steady and keeping it simple. He is one of those guys who is rich in the things that truly matter. You are fascinating and frightening. The life of risk taking that you have chosen is brave and exciting. I wonder if you ever wish you could back up and drop the whole plan to just enjoy golfing, being rich and taking it easy.

I'm exhausted trying to keep up with you. My cousins happily spend their days playing word games with their friends. I am still trying to change the world. Good or bad? I am not sure. It is what it is.

MUSIC AND MAYHEM

August 16, 2018

Dear Donald,

    I am holding my breath today. Aretha Franklin is eating up a lot of the morning news. She was a tower of talent and success. The country hails her accomplishments and mourns her loss. She passed on August 16th which was the same day that Elvis died. Last year, I sat in the Rock and Roll Hall of Fame here in Cleveland and listened to all of Elvis's music. I had not been a fan in my youth, but now as a grandmother, I marveled at his immense talent and was moved deeply by his spiritual recordings. A few years ago, I saw a theater production about Janis Joplin. I was stunned at how impressed I was with her songs and performances. I awakened to her profound talent. I haven't paid much attention to Aretha but I was moved by the coverage of her career today and I will look for more opportunities to hear her music.

    Today, I am also deeply attuned to the politics of the day. Never in my life was I so involved in following so many local, state, national and international concerns. There are aspects of your very frank ways of speaking that continue to make me cringe one moment and shake my head the next. You are a worldly man and every sin you might ever have committed is magnified and publicized and perhaps exaggerated.

The abuse of children who were victimized by so many priests is horrifying. The Manafort trial has concluded and the jury will make a decision today. The trial seems dirty to me in every way. The prosecution is manipulative and self-serving and Manafort certainly is no saint. I don't think any of it should keep him in prison forever.

Christopher Watts in Colorado killed his pregnant wife and two small children. Now that is the worst thing I heard today. Turkey is defying us and Iran is showing no hope of coming around. Omarosa is threatening all kinds of trouble. Canada is not yet at the table regarding trade wars. China is bucking us. Mexico may be ready to sign a trade deal. What happened to Russia?

I am doing my best to take care of myself so I can devote my time to following the news on every level of politics. You did this to me. There was something about your brave, brash bold demand to make America great again. I believe each of us should own the responsibility to take care of what we can to the best of our ability. I think I am doing that by listening, looking, caring and confronting one crazy issue at a time.

PAIN, PAIN, PAIN

August 22, 2018

Dear Donald,

Pain, Pain, Pain. Dale is suffering on and off with a kidney stone, mostly on. The agony of watching him, hour after hour in extreme discomfort has me emotionally paralyzed. I am afraid to be away from the house leaving him alone. Getting him to a doctor or hospital is daunting. I managed to get him to the hospital a few days ago and only because his pain was utterly unbearable. Now, it comes and goes. He is on very heavy medication and until this situation is resolved, I am stuck. I don't know what to do? I take care of him and worry so much that I have to "shake it off" so that I can function.

The whole Michael Cohen and Paul Manafort ordeal has to feel like a kidney stone for you. No! Not for you! You are impervious. You go from New York to Washington to West Virginia to who knows where next and stay calm, cheerful and defiant. In the meantime, it seems like the television programming is all about who is guilty here, there and everywhere. My guess is that we're all a little guilty of something. It scares me to listen to all of it. Even the Catholic Church has been found horribly, shockingly, devastatingly guilty.

The young girl Molly, in Iowa, has at last been found. She was apparently murdered by an illegal alien. I hate this immigrant problem. I don't want any of the really good people who are here illegally to suffer and I sure don't want the bad people to get away with murder. I am praying that we can resolve the border issues and stop fighting one another about it.

I had to turn the TV off today. The negative noise is blaring all day and night. You talk on top of it and drown it out with the insistent cry that we are going to make America great again. You are solving the problems of the world, my friend, while Dale and I are just trying to get through the day.

I got into my size 8 dress easily and it looks great. I am ready for the wedding we had planned to attend in Chicago, but we didn't plan on kidney stones. These are our big issues for the moment and they seem huge to us. Packing, unpacking, feeling better, feeling worse, going to emergency rooms and doctors and then to work and then maybe not, watching and waiting for pain. How do you do it, Donald? Every minute of every day of your life you have to be on guard for the next attack. And yet, you stand tall, tweet endlessly and insist incessantly that you're the ultimate fixer, that you are going to take all the pain away.

TELL ME AGAIN AND AGAIN

September 7, 2018

Dear Donald,

You are in Fargo, North Dakota today and a coal mining executive joined you at the podium with tears in his eyes and a quivering voice. He is grateful for what you have done to bring back the coal industry. You have been going to state after state campaigning for Republicans who are running for office in the upcoming election. I listen to you say the same things over and over, speech after speech, state after state and I never tire of it. I love the way you speak. I taught many subjects when I taught school and Speech was one of them. I was valedictorian of my high school class, an English, Speech and Drama teacher, a television talk show producer and host. Public speaking is my thing. I must say I enjoyed the eloquence of Obama for a long time, but not nearly as much as I enjoy listening to you speak.

What is it that I admire so much about your eloquence? I love that when you speak, you are real, simple, understandable, relatable, excited and tireless. You are proud, passionate and focused. You are relaxed. There is nothing stiff about your presentation. You are having fun. You are energizing. I have to admit that I love watching you arrive in your jet. I am thrilled by the consistently huge crowds that show up at stadiums and large venues for your talks. An audience of at least ten thousand is not unusual. You are excited about your mission and I am excited about your mission too.

I am nearly finished with my first DEAR DONALD book and now I am learning how to publish and promote it. I hope someday you will have copies of this one and the three more that I intend to write about you.

A picture was taken of me at a wedding in Chicago last week and I was wearing red white and blue. It was not a conscious choice, but I loved that it was taken on Labor Day. Perfect. Of course, it also helped that it was a "good hair" day and I looked pretty thin. Nothing is worse than having your friends send photos everywhere that make you look awful and fat. I think I may use the shot on the back cover of my book.

Thank you for inspiring me. I do not have any writer's block when it comes to you. To me, you are "Dear Donald" every day. You are far from perfect, but I love you anyway. Keep making America Great.

FINALLY KAVANAUGH

October 8, 2018

Dear Donald,

Your Topeka, Kansas rally attracted more than 11,000 fans. You enthusiastically celebrated the positive vote for Kavanaugh for the Supreme Court. Will this positive energy in your base continue to insure more Republicans win seats in the Senate in the mid-terms in thirty days?

The polls are showing a significant increase in Republican support. The accusations and public inquiry of Kavanaugh's supposed sexual misconduct were heartbreaking, humiliating and infuriating. In the end, the final Senate vote affirmed his confirmation. There is no way to measure the grief and sadness this spectacle provoked. The malice was unjust and the search for truth was used in a way that hurt everyone.

Doug Schoen defends the Democrats and assures the public that only a small group of them are focusing on the impeachment of the President and now Supreme Court Judge Kavanaugh. My friends and family were glued to the television screens throughout this agonizing spectacle. It is necessary to continue to educate ourselves and to vote our values. Peacefully reaching out to our friends and family who differ with us politically is another positive action. Today's political tone needs to change and the desire to work together constructively must find a place in politics.

Thank heavens for the remarkable speech given by Susan Collins emphasizing that Americans are innocent until proven guilty. Bravo to Lindsey Graham for his unapologetic, furious and passionate defense of Kavanaugh. Mitch McConnell outdid himself as he remained impervious, strong and steady. But most of all, I was grateful for the heart wrenching statement from Kavanaugh, himself.

This awful ordeal motivated Americans. Sadly, it moved some to ugly protest. The "swamp" is everywhere in Washington on both sides of the aisle. God bless you Mr. President for taking it on. God help you!

DREAM COME TRUE

_____

October 12, 2018

Dear Donald,

I am catching up on my writing to you and enjoying looking over my notes. While so many of my subjects are serious, tragic, dangerous, contentious and threatening, it is no wonder that I am so delighted to laugh and smile watching Kanye West's visit to you at the White House. It was adorable. I felt such joy at his enthusiasm and delight. He was candid and honest in sharing his feelings. He was hopeful and positive. He was happy and excited. He hugged you. For one brief moment, I felt there was hope for the world. He was bold and brave. He expressed his honest emotions.

Kanye melted my heart and yours too, I think. There was love in the room. It was palpable. One young female commentator later said she wanted to shoot the feelings in that room into her veins. You were, for a moment, embraced and appreciated by a powerful black man for your support of the black community. "I love you!" he said, and my eyes filled with tears. He wanted to set up a meeting with you and Colin Kaepernick. Crazy? I think it was the sanest statement that I have heard in a long time.

He wants to talk to you and work with you on prison reform, mental illness, drugs, jobs and the 4th amendment. He praised your accomplishments and offered support to improve relations between black and white populations. "The only moment we have is NOW!" This is what he said and I was thrilled to hear it. He did not want the black community to dwell on the past, but to work with you to continue to change the present. It is important to advance the success of all groups, including minorities.

I wanted to shout "Kanye, I love you." Why can't we all be full of joy and praise and hope and spontaneous optimism like you? This was a magical moment quickly seized upon and sabotaged by the opposition. I am saddened by this. Come back, Kanye. Don't doubt your love or optimism. You are a force for hope in an America in desperate need of reconciliation between parties, races and genders.

Donald, I hope you will welcome him back. There was love in the air for a beautiful moment.

MERCILESS MURDER

October 15, 2018

Dear Donald,

We are all waiting to see how our government will respond to the brutal murder of Saudi Arabian journalist Jamal Khashoggi. By American standards, Khashoggi's critical comments about the Saudi were fairly moderate. It has become verified, however, that he was brutally killed and dismembered by Saudis. It remains unclear just how involved the Royal Prince was in instigating this assassination. The Saudi foreign minister claims the incident was a tremendous mistake made by a rogue operation gone wrong. The Saudi leaders want to be deemed innocent until proven guilty. They promise that those responsible will be punished.

The world watches in horror, aghast at the extreme cruelty of the event. You, Donald, are deeply concerned and must make careful decisions about how the United States will respond to this travesty. Khashoggi was a respected journalist in the US. There is no tolerance for freedom of the press in Saudi Arabia. The Saudi foreign minister would refute that, and he vows to get to the bottom of this event, which he says was not authorized by Saudi leaders.

You are carefully measuring your response as you have worked so hard to build a positive relationship with the Saudi government and have negotiated huge deals with them that effect hundreds of thousands of American jobs. This event sabotages so much of your hard work and good will toward the Saudis. There are no quick fixes to this. It is your hope that your relationship with the Saudi government will weather this terrible storm.

"Mercy" is a complicated issue here. You are careful not to overreact or to under react to this outrageous event. You urge that patience be embraced while exhaustive investigation of the incident by many governments embarks. You are stoic and steady in the midst of a tragic and shocking incident. This work makes presidents age quickly. I pray for you. I pray that you continue to be blessed with renewed strength, longevity and a strong heart.

GOOD NEWS

October 17, 2018

Dear Donald,

There was good news this week! I was weeping as I watched you welcome Pastor Andrew Brunson back into the US at the White House. Christians around the world wept with me. He had been imprisoned in Turkey for two years and was facing a thirty-five-year sentence for treason. You stand firmly against foreign entities holding hostages and pressuring the United States for outlandish ransoms. You have brought many such hostages home with your strong stands and effective diplomacy.

The welcoming of Pastor Brunson, his wife and children into the White House was heartwarming. His family was so deeply grateful and moved by your efforts and your success in obtaining his release. He knelt before you and laid hands on you, blessed you, and called for God to fill you with wisdom and strength. Pastor Brunson's wife then raised her hands in praise extending the prayer and blessings. This sacred moment touched me deeply.

There will be more good news. There will be more fairness

and peace. There will be the abolishment of chemical weapons, an end to homelessness, drug addiction, illegal immigration and joblessness. We will work across the aisle to find solutions to our health care issues and rebuild the infrastructure. US schools will be improved and will rank among the best in the world. The family unit will be strengthened and a solution will be found for this epidemic of forest fires in California. We must fight for the rights of everyone, including the unborn, while still preserving personal choices and freedoms. It is necessary to educate and inspire rather than legislate and repress. Can we end world hunger? Can we control devastating storms, earthquakes and devastating fires?

These dreams seem possible when a moment of miraculous spirit permeates the West Wing. One man's perfect prayer makes us believe that all things are possible.

YEARNING

_____

November 10, 2018

Dear Donald,

Droves of people from Honduras, Guatemala, and Nicaragua
are heading our way. They seem young and strong. They are
"yearning to breathe free" and want to storm the "gates of
heaven" and claim asylum in the United States. Many seekers
seem angry and obstinate. Some are violent. They seem willing
to fight their way in. Among the men, there are some women
and children at the front of a mob of thousands. At first, it was
a few thousand. According to one report, the crowd has grown
to around fourteen thousand! Another report is that the number
is dwindling from fatigue. I am sad and angry and afraid and
confused.

Day after day, mobs of angry people are fighting your every
move. I don't know how you manage the horror of this. You fight
the tariffs from nations around the world, the high taxes for the
middle class, the lack of respect and support for the military and
police, the endless investigations against you and anyone near

you, fake news, propaganda, corruption and ISIS. Now, you must fight the migrant mob.

They are yearning to be in the United States. They do not want to be in Mexico. It is said that around the world, 179 million people want to emigrate to the United States. With all of our flaws, we are still the wonder of the world. You are taking this on and I am watching with awe. This problem which has been incessant for many years is one that you are determined to solve. I trust you to be strong and humane.

Americans are yearning also to see our citizens working and making good wages. We want to invest in infrastructure, to pay down our deficit and establish better health care for those who are here. Our doors welcome those who come into our country legally. We want to be generous and supportive, but we do not want to be taken advantage of, used or scorned. We want to help. We do help. But we no longer will be trampled. We want to be respected.

FIRE EVERYWHERE

_____

November 13, 2018

Dear Donald,

Today, it seems that fire is burning everywhere. I despair at the raging inferno in California and, like you, I am angry. These fires never seem to stop and they are devastating. Is there anything that we can do to stop them? With technology, is it possible to change the wind or the weather? Is it climate change? Or poor forest and water management?

The pain and suffering is stunning. The loss of life, destruction of property and incinerations of entire towns has the state and the nation grieving. Day after day, the fires rage out of control and sweep across the state like a demon from Hell. This seems to happen again and again and all of us are desperate to find a way to prevent it. Although forest fires are sometimes important for the forest ecosystem, they are now in populated areas and need to be fought. We can go to the moon, but we cannot control the fires on the earth.

These are the deadliest fires in the state's history. We need a rainmaker. Is the dry weather the only culprit here? Is the wind the evil doer? I fear that there is a plot undiscovered, a bad guy undetected, a cause not considered. I fear inadequate prevention. Donald, you think it might be from poor forest management and the rerouting of water to prevent extinction of a species. Others deny that and blame climate change. Whatever the cause, we feel so helpless and overwhelmed by this that we hunt for a culprit to pin this on. Butte County sheriff speaks to news outlets with a sad and broken voice. I hear his heavy heart.

There are "firestorms" everywhere, not just in California. Kashoggi's brutal murder is still in the news along with the heinous sexual abuses in the Catholic Church, the unsettled elections and the smoldering rage between political parties.

Veteran's Day offered a moment of healing balm. Congressman elect Crenshaw, a handsome and seemingly very kind and gentle man, visited the set of Saturday Night Live. He extended good wishes to comedian Pete Davidson who had made some unkind jokes about him. Wearing a patch over his right eye due to a battle injury, Crenshaw made light of Davidson's bad joke and the two had fun together on camera. Davidson's apology was sweet. Both men succeeded in putting out a potential "firestorm" with a moment of levity and grace.

THANKSGIVING

_____

November 18, 2018

Dear Donald,

Your leadership inspired me to become more involved in American politics. This has been an enormous journey for me as I continue to learn about our government and all the issues facing our nation. I am grateful for the vibrant economy, the firm establishment of fair trade around the world, the conquering of ISIS, the efforts to strengthen the border and to maintain a legal system of immigration. I am so glad the Supreme Court nomination finally was a success for you.

We need to do more with healthcare reform. We need to handle the issue of pre-existing conditions. We will. I have faith that you will find a way to work with Nancy Pelosi, if elected, and Chuck Schumer in the House. You agree with many Democrats on issues related to pharmaceuticals and infrastructure. I thank God for all that you did to hold the Senate.

I am thankful for your strength and have not been as much put off by your "rough" and sometimes negative tone as many suburban women have. My father was a "tough guy" so to speak, and I fought my way past his heavy hand into his extremely soft heart. I know that you are capable of changing your tone and of being more optimistic. I trust that you will get there.

The mistakes that fueled the California fires infuriate you, and yet when you walk about the carnage, you offer whatever support is necessary to help California. Mobs of migrants threaten our borders. While you stand firmly with our immigration laws, while you agree that your wife should embrace the children and reach out with compassion towards those who want to come to America. I see you as a knight who draws his sword in battle and at the same time, opens his heart to his people. My father would approve of the 13th century Persian poem by Saadi, Outside the City Walls:

> All men and women are to each other
> The limbs of a single body, each of us drawn
> From life's shimmering essence, God's perfect pearl;
> And when this life we share wounds one of us
> All share the hurt as if it were our own.
> You, who will not feel another's pain,
> You forfeit the right to be called human.

I trust you as a warrior and pray that you will get to a place where you feel it is safe to show your tender heart.

GOODBYE WITH A LITTLE HELLO IN IT

December 5, 2018

Dear Donald,

Today, we celebrated the life of a very great man, President George H.W. Bush. I have embraced every moment of his eulogies for days now and I am moved. He was indeed a power of example, as he lived a life of love and forgiveness. Thank heavens that you are able to be included in this sacred event and that you and Melania are reaching out to the Bush family and are being respectfully received.

Your campaign was ruthless and the pains inflicted on both sides, are not easily transcended. My son is watching. He commented to me about Bush Sr., "They don't make 'em like that anymore." I am glad that he can observe the example that this man was to all of us. For today at least, all of us, no matter what our politics, can recognize and humbly appreciate goodness.

The living Presidents are seated in the front row. There is

---

tension there and unsettled rivalry. Stubbornly and relentlessly, the spirit of this President you have all come to bury pleads to you. The repeated remembrances of his exemplary life are like the velvet hammer that was used to describe his mother. Bush Senior reached out to his ruthless rival, Bill Clinton and they became friends. All things are possible.

Bush Sr. says goodbye to us and hello to his beloved Barbara and long missed daughter, Robbin. "Ceiling and visibility unlimited." I hope you are inspired and encouraged by this event. It is special. It is a gift to all of us.

SYRIAN SHOCK AND WALL WOES

December 20, 2018

Dear Donald,

Your decision to pull out all of our troops from Syria is being overwhelmingly disapproved of by the House and the Senate. Putin loves the idea. That in itself concerns me. I am not an expert on international affairs but I am listening carefully to all of the experts and I am baffled by this decision that you are making.

On the other hand, I am very impressed with the deals you are making with Mexico and amazed that you have negotiated that all asylum seekers who are at our border, but still bunkered down in Mexico, will not be let into the US. They will proceed with asylum trials while staying in Mexico. This is a wonderful decision and solves the nightmare of those who enter the US seeking asylum, only to disappear into the country never to return for their scheduled hearings. This negotiation with Mexico on your part was brilliant and solves so many problems. You are fighting for a Wall...physical, electronic and military. I am glad you have negotiated with Mexico for an unexpected solution to what feels to so many American citizens like an invasion.

Lindsay Graham and Marco Rubio, among many others, plead that you change your mind on the issue of Syria. They feel that the Syrians you leave behind will be slaughtered and that no one in the Middle East will work with us again.

The Democrats have built a "wall" of their own as they do not support you regardless of what you request, even if you ask for things that they were in total agreement about when Obama was President. Shumer, Hillary Clinton and Obama all agreed that a wall and many other implementations of border security were desperately needed at the border. Israel tells us that a proper wall secures their country from invasion and illegal immigration. Many in the US say immigrants use ladders and tunnels to avert the walls. We long for some consensus. The one wall that we do not need is the one between Republicans and Democrats.

THE NIGHT BEFORE CHRISTMAS

December 24, 2018

Dear Donald,

We are about to celebrate Christmas Eve. I will not be a Scrooge. I am listening to Jason Chaffetz and grateful that he is emphatically defending your stand on building whatever the border patrol is requesting. The border patrol wants comprehensive border patrol and they want, in appropriate places, a border fence. Five billion dollars is not enough. The Democrats are fixated on making you wrong. You are dug in. You'll figure this out, Donald. I trust that. I pray for that.

I worry about Syria and Afghanistan. Your decisions on these issues frighten me, but that doesn't mean that they are wrong. There is always a method to your madness. Will the real "mad dog" please stand up? I worry about the stock market. The entire country seems to be too busy shopping to do much about all of these issues. Christmas looms large and glorious, as the nation chooses to lean on the good financial news of most of 2018. It is as though we are all counting on a Christmas miracle to right the ship. The current financial weather outside is frightful, but our Christmas fantasies are delightful and we will not give up our "merry" to cow tow to political madness.

Your opposition is lining up for the 2020 race. Despite the tumultuous week that we have had around the world, I am confident that you will win again in 2020. Upheaval is a part of your DNA. Building is your thing and that is what you are doing, brick by brick. You always manage to finish a project before deadline and under budget.

Just spoke to Dale's daughter in California and warned her that I am about to release this book. I know that California is very liberal and she is a "California" girl for sure. She lives on her boat! I was surprised at her response to my Dear Donald book. She said that she thinks that you are a little "looney", but in a way you are saving us. I never expected that kind of a response from her. She is not alone. Millions who support you don't let on to anyone around them that they do. There are prayers of support engulfing you and yours from unexpected places far and near. God Bless you Donald and Merry, Merry Christmas.

About the Author

Sandra Lee is an award-winning author, magazine publisher, television personality, educator, songwriter, and artist with a Master's Degree in Visual and Performing Arts. Sandra is a native of Northeastern Ohio, where she now makes her home after having lived and worked in the New York metro area for most of professional career.

She encapsulates the independent-minded modern woman whose swing votes are coveted by both Democrats and Republicans.

Follow on Facebook:: www.facebook.com/deardonaldbooks
Follow on Twitter:: twitter.com/deardonaldbooks
Email:: SandraLee@deardonaldbooks.com
Website:: www.deardonaldbooks.com

CPSIA information can be obtained
at www.ICGtesting.com
Printed in the USA
BVHW081234040219
539400BV00003B/281/P

9 780996 620833